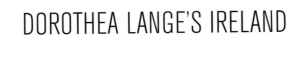

DOROTHEA LANGE'S IRELAND

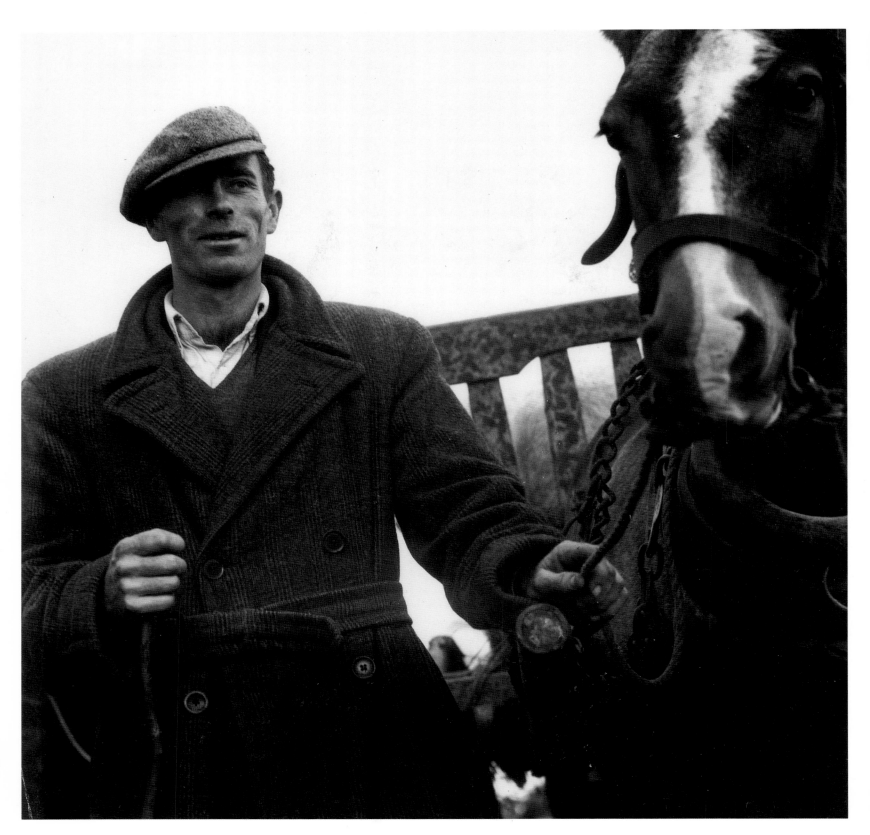

DOROTHEA LANGE'S
IRELAND

Text by Gerry Mullins

Essay by Daniel Dixon

Photographs from the collection of
The Oakland Museum of California

ELLIOTT & CLARK PUBLISHING
Washington, D.C.

ACKNOWLEDGMENTS

This project was greatly enhanced by the goodwill of a large number of people,
a small group of whom I would like to acknowledge: Emma Curley and Peter Curley
for valued friendships; Drew Johnson at the Oakland Museum for enormous patience;
Gael editor Raymond Hughes for the opportunity to first approach this project;
photographer Rory McNamara for technical support; Betsy Partridge for her
"been there" words of wisdom; Anne Heraty for tireless research work in County Clare;
John Meere of the Four Winds guest house in Ennis for his local knowledge;
Daniel Dixon, Michael Kenneally, Maureen Niedzialkoski, Robert Tottenham, and
Dennis Wylde for generously sharing their memories; the staff of the Department of
Rural Development at University College Dublin for support; publisher Carolyn Clark for
her expertise; and my parents Kitty and Maurice for advice on much of this text. —G.M.

(Page 2) A farmer at Tubber fair.

Edited by Elizabeth Brown Lockman. Designed by Gibson Parsons Design.
Photo edited by Gerry Mullins and Carolyn Clark. Photographic prints by Edward and Elfriede Dyba.
Printed and bound in Hong Kong through Mandarin Offset.

10 9 8 7 6 5 4 3 2 1   2001 2000 1999 1998 1997 1996

Library of Congress Cataloging-in-Publication Data

Lange, Dorothea.
Dorothea Lange's Ireland / text by Gerry Mullins ; essay by Daniel Dixon ;
Photographs from the collection of the Oakland Museum.
p.   cm.
ISBN 1-880216-35-3
I. Ireland—Pictorial works.   I. Mullins, Gerry, 1970– .   II. Oakland Museum.   III. Title.
DA978.L96 1996
941.5'009734'0222—dc20   95-38835
                                                          CIP

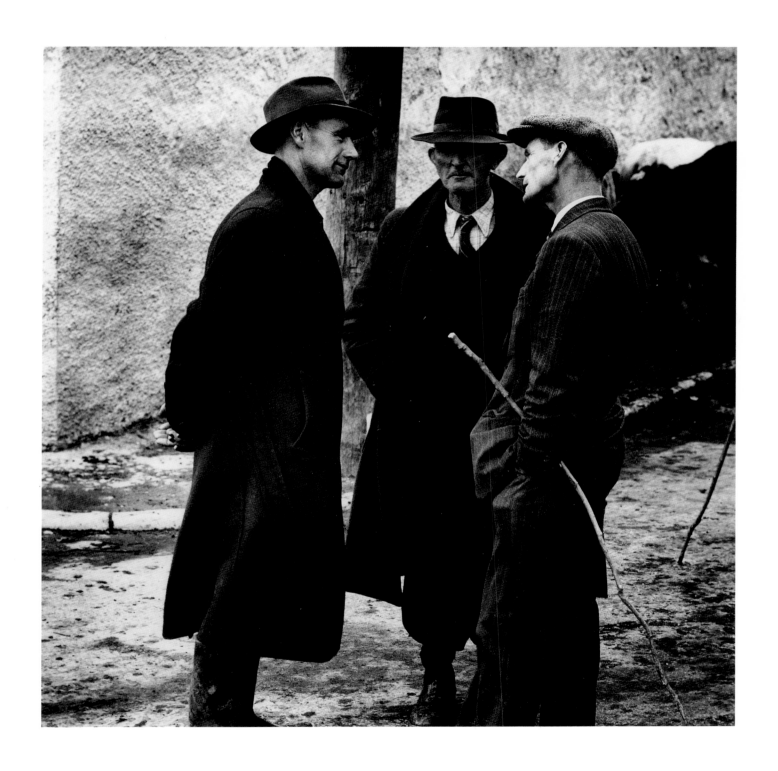

Cattlemen talk shop at the fair at Sixmilebridge.

DOROTHEA LANGE'S IRELAND

Dorothea Lange was not an avid reader. But among the few books which became her favorites was a description of the sort of culture that drew her attention time and again throughout her career, a rural society where customs, beliefs, and the way of life itself were tied to the soil.

The book was called *The Irish Countryman*. Written in 1937 by a young anthropologist from Harvard, Conrad Arensberg, it documented and analyzed the social and economic traditions of Irish rural life and discussed how they were affected by religion and superstition. In it, Arensberg located the family farm at the hub of this complex system and explained how each generation placed an overriding importance on "keeping the [family] name on the land."

The rural Irish family was supported by a system of kinship and friendship, which in this context were practically synonymous. One important element in this system was the custom of "cooring," from the Irish word *comhair*, which means "to help." If, for example, the mother in a neighboring house was ill, a daughter would be sent to help with family chores until the mother was well again. Another example was when women in a village pooled their resources to make a firkin of butter.

"Lending a boy" was the most common form of cooring. It was most visible at recurring occasions of great activity such as "saving the hay." During the mowing, stacking, and moving of this essential crop, boys from families that did not own mowing machines often worked free of charge for a local farmer who had such equipment. His hay harvested, the host farmer then paid his debt by mowing the meadows of the farmers whose sons had helped him.

The way of life described by Arensberg contrasted sharply with the plight of migrant farmers photographed by Lange in California during the 1930s. She deplored the grim cycle of natural and financial disasters that had made nomads of farmers and their families during the Great Depression. Describing the process as "wiping the people from the land," she said that it was "harmful to family relationships, and the family unit, and was tantamount to unraveling the fabric of America." She believed that the exodus of people from their homes and the land that they owned was "eroding the humanity of the United States."

In 1954 Dorothea Lange traveled to Ireland where, to her mind, the humanity had remained fully intact. Earlier that year, Lange had decided that she wanted to photograph the kinds of scenes and people Arensberg had described, and she had obtained an agreement from *Life* magazine to sponsor her trip. Traveling with her was her son, Daniel Dixon. Just as the pair had worked together a year earlier in Utah, studying Mormon society, Dorothea would take the pictures for the photographic essay, while Daniel would write the narrative.

Lange and Dixon arrived in Dublin in early September. They spent a couple of days photographing the environs of Trinity College and St. Stephen's Green and visited the Folklore Commission at St. Stephen's Place. They then headed west to County Clare.

It was in the 26-house village of Luogh in County Clare that Arensberg had lived for two years while researching his book, *The Irish Countryman*. Arensberg chose Clare because it offered "a blending of older Gaelic and modern British influences, and one that was neither entirely Gaelic nor entirely English in speech." Much of the land is poor there, and the farms are generally small. (During the 1950s more than half of all farms were between 15 and 50 acres.) Clare also had a strong cultural profile. It remains the home of Irish traditional music and is one of the stronger counties in the ancient Irish sport of hurling. Great Irish political leaders Daniel O'Connell and Eamonn de Velera were first elected to Parliament from County Clare. The Home Rule leader Charles Stewart Parnell was a regular visitor to Ennis, the county's principal town. Parnell is believed to have first met Kitty O'Shea's husband, W. H. O'Shea, in a hotel there. The scandal of Parnell's love affair with Kitty ended his political career in 1890. Both Parnell and O'Connell have streets named in their honor in Ennis.

It was not Lange's intention to produce a photographic version of Arensberg's work, but *The Irish Countryman* clearly influenced her choice of subject matter in Ireland. On September 4, using her married name, Dorothea Lange Taylor, she and Dixon checked into two rooms at the Old Ground Hotel in Ennis. Except for a brief visit to Cork city, they stayed in Ennis a month. During this time, she took 2,400 photographs.

In 1954 Ennis had a population of 7,000 and was serviced by dozens of small businesses including 65 pubs. Using the town as a base, Lange photographed Ennis itself and villages throughout County Clare. With Daniel at the wheel of their rented car, they often drove through the countryside, looking for photographic subjects.

On one such occasion near Cloonanaha, about 10 miles west of Ennis, she photographed Michael Kenneally,

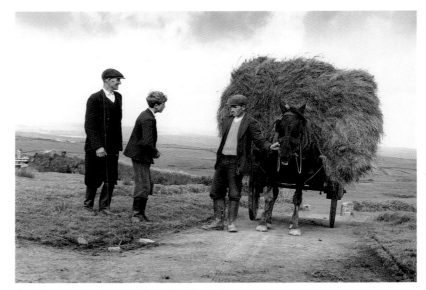

A neighbor pauses for a chat at the O'Halloran farm, Mount Callan.

a young farmer, working in a field near his home. Lange visited the Kenneally farm on several occasions to photograph him and his mother Nora (pages 19–23). "Any time she was passing and saw me working in the fields, she would come up and start clicking away," Kenneally remembers. "In the beginning I would stop and have a chat. But after a while I'd take no notice and keep working."

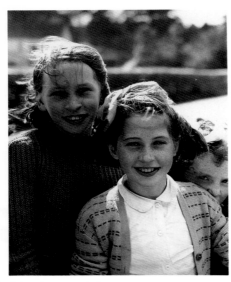

Girls on their way to school.

Lange was clearly interested in people, but she was also interested in their ritualized comings and goings, and chose this as a theme for her work in Ireland. Just as she had been instructed to do in the 1930s by Roy Stryker, her boss at the Farm Security Administration, she photographed people on their way to and from their places of worship: at the Catholic churches at Cloonanaha (pages 24–27) and at Rath (pronounced Ra) five miles from Corofin (page 103). Two other important institutions in the life of the Irish country person were schools and the GAA (Gaelic Athletic Association), and so Lange photographed children on their way to class (pages 32–33) and groups of people at a hurling match in Newmarket-on-Fergus (pages 110–111).

Knowing from Arensberg's book that open-air markets offered a rare opportunity for farmers to receive a cash income, Lange visited the markets at Ennis, Ennistymon, Tubber, and Sixmilebridge (pages 81–93). She also studied dairy farmers taking milk to their local cooperative (pages 48–52). "The creamery," she described in her notes, "is the symbol of Eire [Ireland] in the 1950s."

Another theme important to the story of rural Ireland was emigration. Lange hoped to investigate this by photographing emigrants before they left Ireland and then by following up their stories in later years back in the United States. Although the second part of her project was never realized, the "old country" side of her study yielded some of her more interesting work in Ireland.

Lange was having difficulty with one of her cameras, and so she took it for repair to a young photographer in Ennis named Dennis Wylde. While she was there, she asked if he had taken passport photographs of anybody planning to emigrate to the United States. Wylde gave her the names of two sisters who were due to leave for New York that November.

Maureen and Catherine O'Halloran were employees at the home of Robert Tottenham, whose family had been landlords in the area since the 1820s. The O'Halloran's farm was once part of the Tottenham estate, which occupied most of the barren hillside of Mount Callan. For generations, the O'Hallorans had worked for the Tottenhams.

Lange visited the O'Halloran farm twice and took several hundred pictures of the family (pages 38–45). She recorded scenes inside the house, where the girls' grandmother Ellen, a stooped octogenarian, spent much of her time by the fireplace. On another occasion, Lange took photographs of the family in their yard and at their chores. She also visited Robert Tottenham, who was photographed inside his house and with a team of workers saving hay on part of his 1,200 acres (pages 53–57).

On occasion when Daniel Dixon was unavailable, Lange asked Dennis Wylde to be her driver. The photographer obliged and was with her for much of her time in Clare. He notes that while she was a very nice person in company, she was very determined in her work. He especially remembers how she would tenaciously pursue a shot until she got it right, even if this meant climbing up a tree, standing on top of the car, or returning to the same place day after day. During her stay in Ireland, Lange never used a flash. Instead, she worked in the early morning to make the most of the natural light.

Both Dixon and Lange felt that the essay in *Life* should convey a general atmosphere of Ireland. Names and places were not important as each picture was representative of scenes in other parts of the country. However, back in New York, the editors at *Life* disagreed. They felt that the piece should be strong on details. Shortly after Lange delivered her pictures to *Life*, they sent a set of contact sheets to one of their journalists in London, Beatrice Dobie. Dennis Wylde was hired to help identify the scenes, and for six days Dobie and Wylde drove around County Clare, recording the names and places in Lange's photographs.

Lange was displeased by "Irish Country People," the photographic essay that appeared in the *Life* issue of March 21, 1955. Although she felt that she had come back from Ireland with "a big harvest," the essay featured only 19 of her images. Dixon too was unhappy. The narrative included little of his text, and his name was not on the credits. Lange was so annoyed with the editors at *Life* that she "bent some people there out of shape," according to Dixon. She did not work for the magazine again.

However, she did receive praise for her Irish work. A noted photographer and the editor of *Aperture* magazine, Minor White, wrote to her saying that he had seen the Irish essay while at the dentist's office in New York: "The essay pleases me very much.... It seems to me that you met the various people in a person to person basis.... I feel that I am touching these people, that I am a friend among friends." John Dominis, a friend and veteran photographer with *Life*, also wrote to her, from the *Life* office in Chicago, saying, "Now that is the kind of picture story I like. You showed us what the Irish countryman is. You did not do a picture story on a group of people and simply use the Irish countryman as your subject. Rather, the people were there first and they were a picture story. You put it on film. Very few picture stories accomplish this."

Although Dorothea Lange never returned to Ireland, her archive at the Oakland Museum indicates that she remained interested in Irish affairs and that she collected relevant newspaper clippings. Among these are an account, with pictures, of the 1956 St. Patrick's Day parade in New York and a piece from the *New York Times* of 1957 about air travel and how it had ended the "American wake" in rural areas of Ireland. There are also two articles from the 1960s: a discussion of Premier Sean Lemass' attempts to bring young men and women off the "crowded farms" and into new factories and an essay on Irish industrial policy and the "rationalization" of agriculture.

Most importantly, her archive shows that there remained a personal interaction between Lange and people she met while in Ireland. She kept a list of names and addresses in Clare under the heading "Photos to send; and people to go back to." She also kept a letter she received while she was still in Ireland from Mimi Spillane, an attendant at St. Joseph's Hospital in Ennis and a woman noted for her skill in knitting. Lange had presumably asked her to knit some clothing for her young grandchildren and received the following reply:

My Dear Mrs. Taylor, I got your letter this morning, many thanks. I understand about the time it takes for parcels to go and come from California (I had a cousin there one time R.I.P.). I was thinking if you got the wool yourself before you go back it would be cheaper for yourself, you would need about 10ozs for the child's rig, frock, cap and shorts, about 4oz grey for socks. I could get the colours myself. I am sure you could get the wool in town. … I am sending a little cap I had done, don't send anything for it …. I was very sorry I hadn't something to fit you going home as you seemed so anxious to have some of my work. With best wishes for a safe journey. Yours V Sincerely, Mimi Spillane.

The following year, in 1955, Lange received a letter from Mrs. Nora Kenneally (pages 19–21). Kenneally wrote to her "Dearest friend Mrs. Taylor," and said that she hoped "the visit to Ireland done you good. I may get the sweep stake to travel myself but not that lucky …. It's lovely if we only meet again …. What did you think of Ireland? It's what we call a plain country, still quite happy. It's what one is used to." She finished by saying, "Please God we may meet again in Ireland. The best of luck for Easter, from an old pal, Nora Kenneally."

On February 4, 1956, Mrs. Kenneally wrote again to thank Lange for her Christmas card. She inquired after "our pal Dan Dixon he being so Irish looking" and said that she sent him a card, but didn't know if the address she had was correct. She praised Lange for the photographs that appeared in *Life*, but then asked for a special favor. "Well my friend, as we were so fond of each other parting on that evening with you and Dan … I will please ask you in case any more of the magazines [are published] … I ask you to get me not photographed …. Its alright for Michael [her son] and the young people …. my family were at me to write you, we being such friends."

Lange had been quite happy in the "plain country." She seemed to understand the way of life, and her mood there was buoyant. She said that she was not focusing on the Irish people as individuals, she was more concerned with "a portrait of the country itself, its population, its customs, its mores, its atmosphere, the texture of its life. In these things you don't approach individuals as individuals. You're thinking on a different level." Nevertheless, Dorothea Lange did approach her Irish subjects as individuals. She entered their homes, she knew their names, and she came to know their families and much about their lives. There seemed to be a mutual affinity.

Fortunately, many of the people Lange met in County Clare were available to help research this book

in 1995. Michael Kenneally (pages 19 and 23) was 24 years old when she visited his farm near Cloonanaha. He still lives in the same cottage he shared then with his mother Nora. The farm has grown from 30 to 70 acres, and the thatch on the house and sheds has been replaced by slate. But little else seems to have changed in the landscape Lange photographed more than 40 years ago.

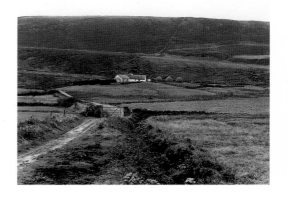

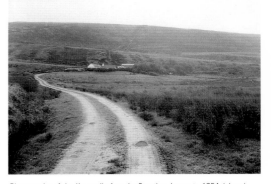

Photographs of the Kenneally farm by Dorothea Lange in 1954 (above) and Gerry Mullins in 1995 (below) show that little of the landscape has changed in 40 years.

Well known in his local community, Kenneally is what the Irish call "a character." Every Christmas for more than 30 years, he has donned a big red suit and white beard and visited each house in the locality, delivering small gifts to young and old alike. Among his lifelong friends is Bridie O'Halloran (page 31), who raised a family eleven miles away in the village of Kilmihil.

By coincidence, several other photographers have visited Michael Kenneally since Lange. When the book series A Day in the Life came to Ireland, Kenneally got an unexpected call from a photographer and film crew. Although he was not included in the book, he appeared in the TV documentary on the making of A Day in the Life of Ireland.

Michael and his wife are now alone in their house, but their adult sons live close by. Their eldest son, also named Michael, is due to take over the farm on his father's retirement. He also has a son named Michael who, according to the present incumbent, will someday inherit the farm. If this happens, the boy will represent the fifth generation with the name Michael Kenneally "on the land." Conrad Arensberg, who now lives in New York, would be pleased that his findings remain valid.

Maureen (page 45) and Catherine O'Halloran (page 42) set sail for the United States out of Queenstown (now called Cobh) two months after Lange photographed them at their home on Mount Callan. They stayed with an aunt in New York for several months, then moved to Worcester, Massachusetts. There they both married and raised a total of six children. They sometimes visit their former home in County Clare, where their eldest brother, Thomas, lives and farms the land.

Robert Tottenham was 29 years old when Lange photographed him. He had inherited the family farm in 1949 and spent 20 years trying to drain the boggy property. Eventually in the early 1970s, he became one of the first Irish farmers to opt for forestry on marginal land. He now has 1,200 acres of sitka spruce and is one of the premier figures in Irish forestry. Married with three sons, he still lives in the same house Lange photographed.

Dennis Wylde, the photographer who worked both with Lange and later for Life magazine on the project, kept in touch with her, and for many years she mailed him copies of American photographic magazines. He says that he learned more about photography from Lange than from any other source. A grandfather now, he is retired and living in Ennis.

Ennis remains a busy small town. Its population has swelled to more than 18,000, and it is now the base of most of the county and state offices. The market still takes place on Saturdays, although some traders open their stalls during the week. Pigs, calves, and vegetables continue to be regular fare, although tool and clock traders now also have stalls. The ivy-covered facade of the Old Ground Hotel has been altered little in the past 40 years. Its interior has been upgraded, and it has changed ownership, but the manager is still able to locate the visitors' book where Dorothea Lange signed her name in 1954.

—*Gerry Mullins*

IRELAND'S DOROTHEA LANGE

The contemplation of things as they are,

Without error or confusion,

Without substitution or imposture,

Is in itself a nobler thing

Than a whole harvest of invention.

This quotation from Sir Francis Bacon was pinned to the wall of my mother's darkroom from the time she first started to photograph in the streets and fields of America during the Great Depression. It served as her professional credo for 35 years. And I think it helps explain why the title of this book might have made her a little uncomfortable.

"Dorothea Lange's Ireland" suggests that the photographer has imposed her own private impressions and interpretations on the country and its people. That was never my mother's purpose. She considered herself a witness, nothing more. To be described as an "artist" made her flinch and squirm. She was the servant rather than the source of her material, and she let her subjects speak for themselves.

The photographs she took in Ireland are eloquent evidence of that fact. Look at these faces, these figures, these landscapes, these towns and country cottages. They are Irish, heart and soul. Nowhere does the American woman behind the camera intrude herself. And in image after image, the people before the camera seem to have composed themselves for their portraits. Their eyes look straight ahead, directly into the lens, secure in their own integrity.

My mother came to Ireland with a deep affection and regard for the Irish people. Her feelings had been strengthened by a slender book called *The Irish Countryman*. Its covers, appropriately, are green. My mother read it many times, and gave me a copy that bears her inscription. "For Dan," it says. "Up the bridge." I never learned the exact meaning of that sentiment, but it sounds hopeful and sympathetic. In fact, it sounds very Irish. In Ireland, I discovered, a man is more apt to be poetic than precise.

The photographic essay called "Irish Country People" was published by *Life* magazine in 1955. I doubt that the editors, normally a flinty and practical group, could have been very enthusiastic about the project. The material was esoteric and of little interest to either the magazine's readers or its advertisers. But this little woman with the limp and the quiet voice and the luminous gray eyes was a persistent and persuasive advocate, and the editors finally yielded to her seductive arts. So off she went to Ireland with her copy of *The Irish Countryman* to serve as a guide and myself to act as researcher, assistant, and possible writer of captions and text.

Our assignment lasted about six weeks. We stopped off in London on the way, but most of our time was spent in County Clare. We lodged at the Old Ground Hotel in Ennis, and the mood of our stay was established on the day we checked in. The day was raw and wet, and our rooms, though comfortable enough, were as cold as Celtic crypts. At the desk, a sturdy young woman accepted our complaint with a confident smile. Her manner suggested that the problem could be fixed with no trouble at all, though I noticed that she was wearing two layers of heavy sweaters. Clucking apologies, she scooted upstairs, twisted some dials, and punished the offending radiators with a few bangs of her wrench. "There you are," she told us. "You'll be having the heat in no time."

It was all a charade, of course. The hotel's heating system was permanently flawed. But that reality didn't affect the young woman's eagerness to make us comfortable, and her attitude was typical. Throughout our assignment, we were chilled by the Irish temperatures but warmed by the Irish temperament.

That was more than 40 years ago, and a fine Irish mist, half rain and half sun, has descended over my memory of names, places, and dates. But here and there the mist suddenly lifts, and there are some incidents that I remember as clearly as though they happened yesterday. "Ireland is always contrary, you know," my mother once said. "But once in a while, the whole earth smiles for a minute, and then it's different."

From the start she seemed to see the Irish people as part of their landscape—living, breathing elements of the earth. One day, standing at the crest of a little hill, we saw a dark figure advancing toward us along a lonely road. Dorothea photographed him at a distance, again as he drew nearer, and finally as he passed us at close range. You can see from these photographs (pages 28–29) why my mother later said, "That's pure Ireland. He was just made out of that wet, limey soil. Made out of it."

And just as she felt these people to be one with their landscape, she also felt them to be one with the Irish weather. We went one day to a remote farm where she photographed the owner standing in his open fields. His body rose from the earth as stubbornly as a rock wall, and he looked as though he'd been carved like a stone by the climate. "That face," my mother said in her notes. "That's the winds of the Atlantic Ocean blowing over it. All his life, never been out of it. Never been out of it."

Whenever she could, my mother took photographs of Irish children—on their way to and from school, running their errands, doing their chores, going to church. She felt that they were incarnations of the past and prophecies of the future. She loved their innocence, and also their mischief. Of one portrait (page 85) she said, "There's a boy there with some sheep, and he has the most wonderful expression on his funny little Irish face." I remember that boy. And I remember the girl (page 31) that she afterward described with a quotation from an Irish poet: "There's been nothing like her since the flight of the wild geese."

My mother carried her cameras almost everywhere. Her energy seemed endless and her interest infinite. We worked on the farms, in the cottages, at the fairs, in the markets, in the shops, along the streets, in the churches and schools. She photographed the wild wandering tinkers, the shawlies with a drop taken, the headstones in the graveyards, the black broken teeth of ruined castles, the coarse cloth caps that were worn like an emblem by almost every Irish countryman. And she also photographed their thick woolen suits. These men commonly owned two such suits—one for Sunday, the other for every other day in the week. The everyday suit smelled of dung and sweat and tobacco and beer and peat. It smelled, in fact, like a compost pit. My mother's photographs defined the queer stubborn dignity of those suits, but not their rich fragrance. Not even Dorothea Lange could photograph an odor.

On one rainy day toward the end of our assignment, we went to a sort of workhouse in Ennis. It was a bleak brick building right out of Dickens, with long dark corridors and grim chambers festooned with cobwebs. There we bought a scrap of handmade lace from a cheerful old woman who earned a bit of money now and again from visitors like ourselves. For years afterward my mother sent

her a gift of cash at Christmas. In return she received from the workhouse a piece of lace and a formal note of thanks and good wishes, until at last the lace and the notes ceased to come.

There was, however, one notable feature of Irish life that my mother left unexplored. Always on distant terms with alcohol, she didn't spend much time or expose much film in the pubs. That was an omission I did my best to correct, though not with my mother's approval. After she went to bed, I'd go down to the bar and roister the bar and roister

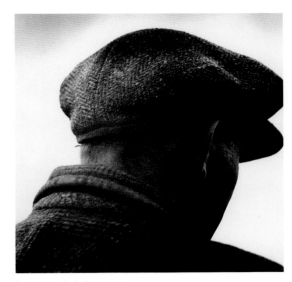

The cap worn by Irish countrymen.

with the locals until closing time. An hour or two later, the "bona fides" would straggle in—dedicated drinkers who could still be legally served because they lived more than three miles away and were therefore considered legitimate travelers. Some of them had been so driven by thirst that they'd pedalled through the dark night on bicycles from neighboring villages. Oh, they had marvelous stories to tell, those bona fides. After one all-night session, I recall

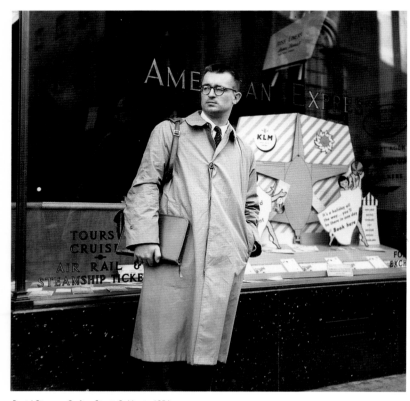

Daniel Dixon on Grafton Street, Dublin, in 1954.

meeting my mother for breakfast without ever having slept. Two of my drinking companions were at an adjoining table, doing their drunken best to spoon oatmeal into their mouths. "Ah, it's you, Dan," they greeted me. "It's a grand time we had together last night. Will you not be comin' to visit us as soon as the humor is on you?"

The humor, alas, was never on me for the rest of our stay in County Clare. The look of frozen rebuke on my mother's face took care of that, all right.

I've never learned to take photographs. My mother

was far too formidable a competitor. But every once in a while she'd hand me a fully loaded camera and encourage me to fire away. That's exactly what happened one market day in Tubber. Wet manure oozing into my shoes, I snapped a snaggle-toothed old farmer leering into the camera as he hoisted two struggling sheep into the air, one with each arm. That photograph (page 88) has since been published and republished, and always as my mother's work. But I remember aiming the camera at that leer and those two woebegone sheep, and it pleases me to think that for this one instant I might have been as good a photographer as Dorothea Lange.

Never before had my mother photographed or even traveled outside her own country. But she seemed to have a special feeling for Irish people right from the start. Here in Ireland she was on familiar ground. Like the farmers she'd photographed in the rural south of the United States, the Irish country people were rooted in the land. They were sometimes very poor but rich in faith. Then forces they didn't understand and couldn't control threatened to drive them from their farms and towns and change their lives forever. My mother recognized and respected their strength, their pride, and their pain. She'd seen these things before in her own country. And though she was a stranger in Ireland, she felt that she was among friends.

In one respect, however, the work my mother did

among the Irish people was something new and different—an important departure. Always before she had attempted to document the human condition in single images. Her effort had been to encapsulate the meaning of events or experiences in one photograph. Now, in Ireland, she was beginning to connect one image with the next, to construct sequences, to build a narrative, to tell a story. "I find that it has become instinctive, habitual, *necessary*, to *group* photographs," she wrote. "I used to think in terms of single photographs—the bullseye technique. No more. A photographic statement is what I now reach for. Hence these pairs, like a sentence of two words. Here we can express the relationships, equivalents, contradictions, positives and negatives, etc. etc. Our medium is peculiarly geared for this. (I am just beginning to understand it.)"

I'm delighted that the work my mother did in Ireland so many years ago is now being published. In my opinion, some of her finest photographs are included here. She, I think, felt the same way. While we were editing the first proof sheets, and then when the selected prints began to come out of the darkroom, I remember her saying again and again, "That's Ireland." For years afterward, right up until the day she died, one or another of these photographs was pinned to her studio wall or displayed on a piece of corkboard in the kitchen. "Look at that face," she'd say of a photograph of an Irish girl smiling in the rain (page 30).

"Isn't that a beautiful face? That's Ireland. That's pure Ireland."

Let me repeat what I said at the start. If my mother had lived to see the publication of *Dorothea Lange's Ireland*, she might have protested the title. But I think the book itself would have pleased her very much. She deeply cared about the people she met and came to know in Ireland. And I believe that she'd have liked to send those Irish country people a greeting. She did that with her photographs. But I think she'd also have wanted to say to them, just as she said to me, "Up the bridge."

Whatever *that* means, exactly.

—Daniel Dixon

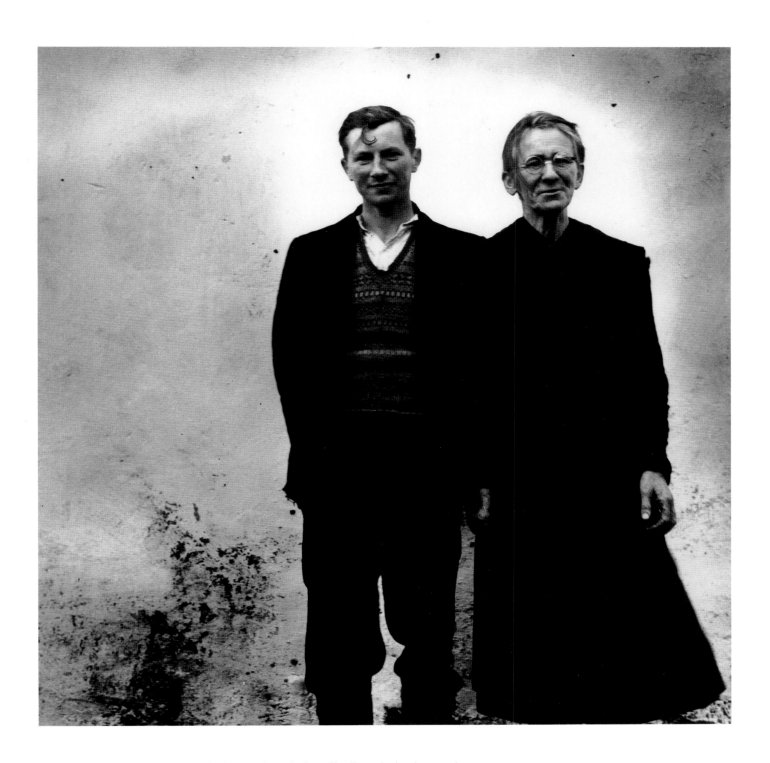

Nora Kenneally with her youngest son Michael at their home near Cloonanaha, County Clare. Her two daughters have married locally, but her three other sons have emigrated, leaving Michael to look after his widowed mother and their farm.

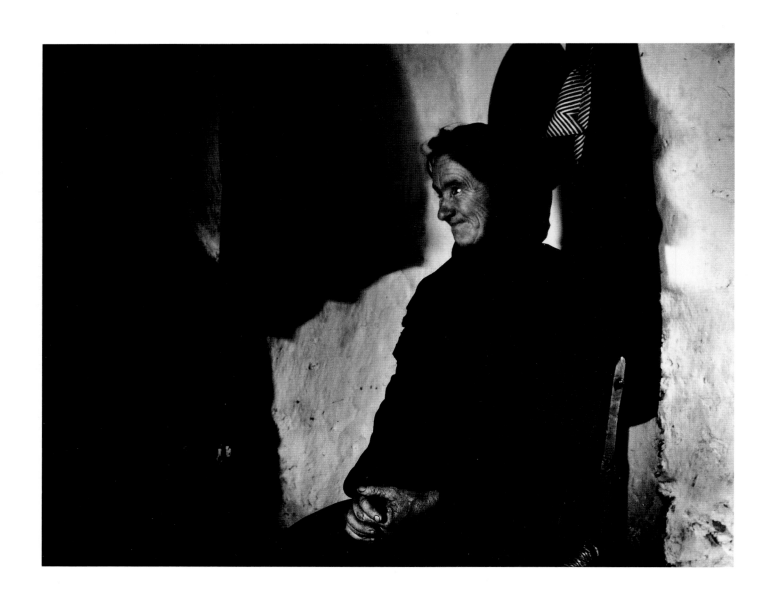

Nora Kenneally at her fireside. Instructing an assistant on how to print this photograph, Lange wrote: "[This picture] was made almost in the dark. Please hype the contrast; never mind that there is nothing in the shadows—watch the face."

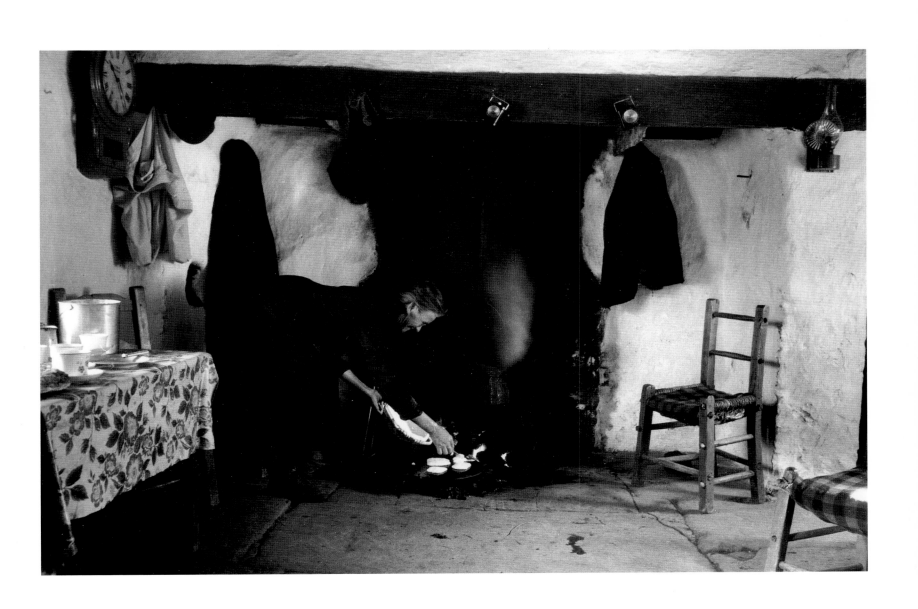

Nora Kenneally prepares potato cakes, a mixture of boiled potatoes, wheat flour, and milk, which
is then heated on a griddle over a turf fire. Traditional Irish sugán chairs made of wood and straw
can be seen to the right.

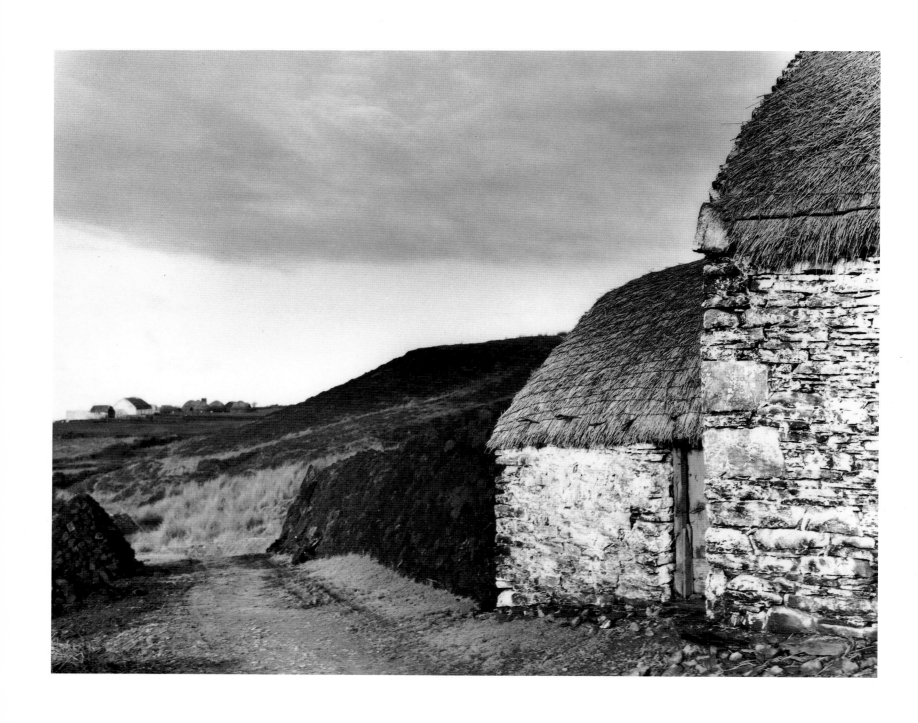

The Kenneally driveway is flanked by stacks of dried turf gathered at a nearby bog, which will serve as fuel during the long, wet winter. The buildings are storage sheds, with thatched roofs and white-washed walls.

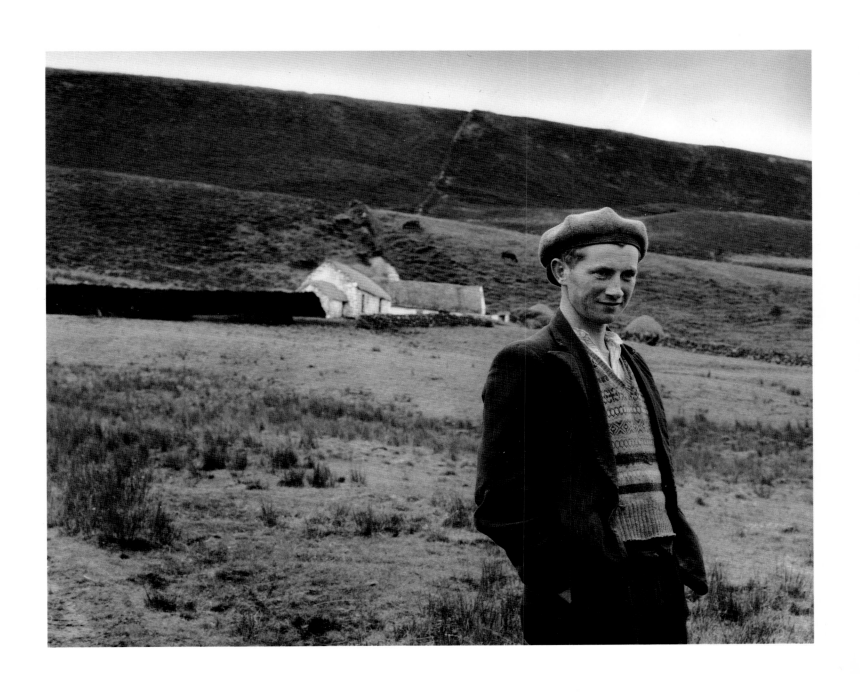

Michael Kenneally on his 30 acres at the brow of Mount Callan. The house
was built by Michael's grandfather.

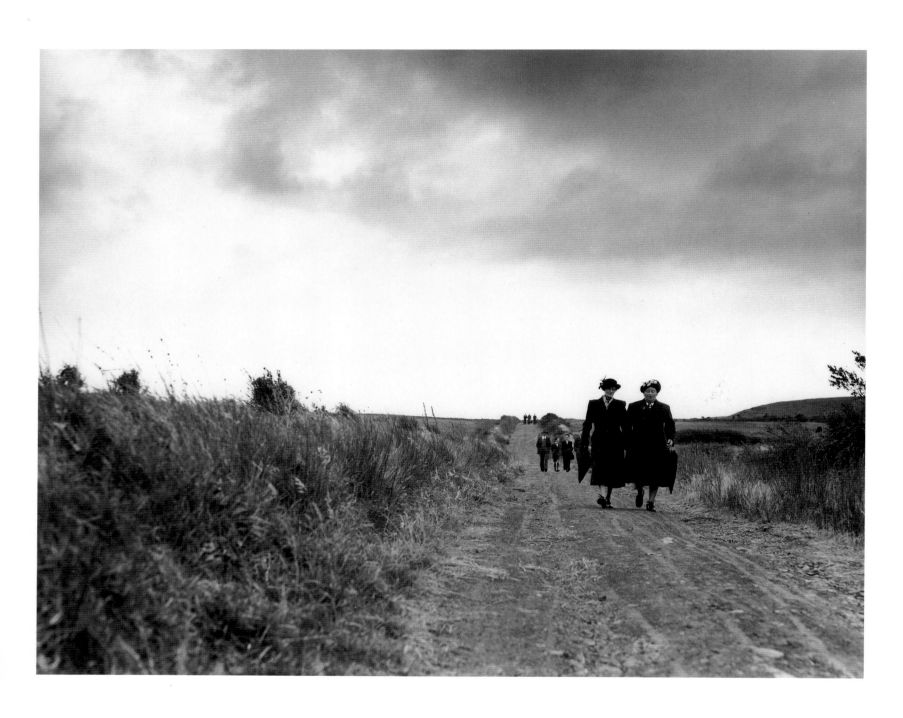

Making their way to Sunday Mass at the parish of Cloonanaha, these women travel seven miles from Mount Callan on bicycles which they then leave at the top of this path. Walking this stretch is preferred to riding on days when the path is muddy.

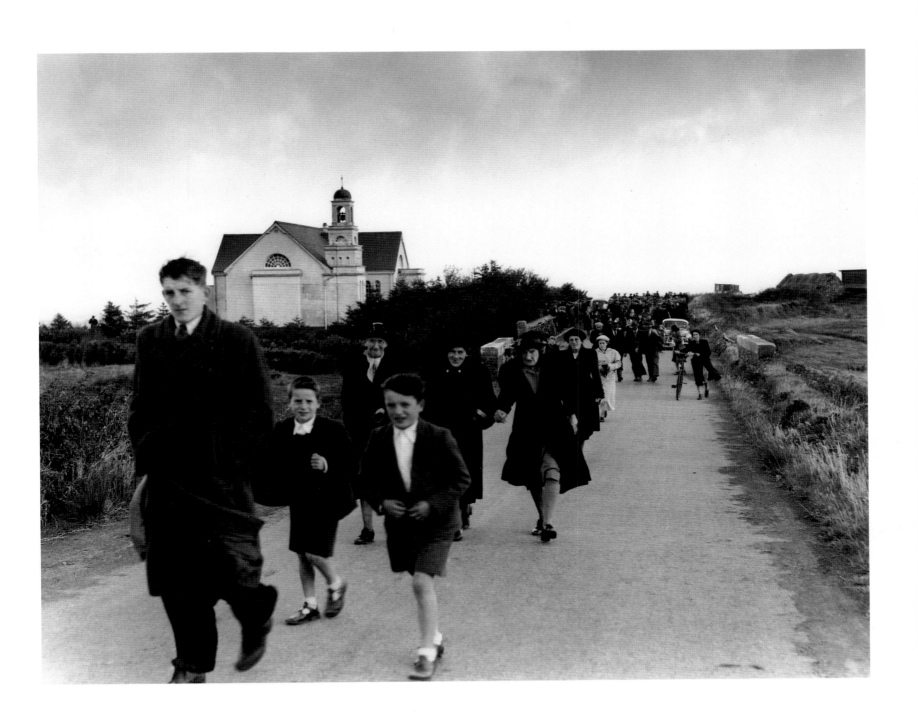

*Many of those leaving Mass have just two sets of clothing, one for regular wear during the week
and the other for Sabbath wear only. The church at Cloonanaha was built in 1937 for IR£2,445
collected by local people, along with donations from the United States.*

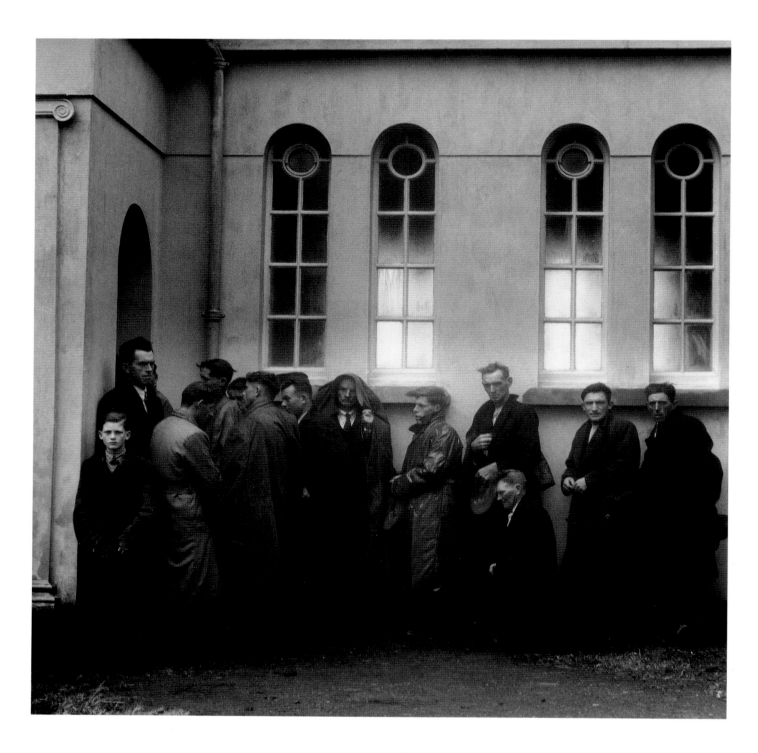

Women and children sit near the altar, while the men take their positions closer to the door.
The single Sunday Mass at St. Mary's is sometimes overcrowded.

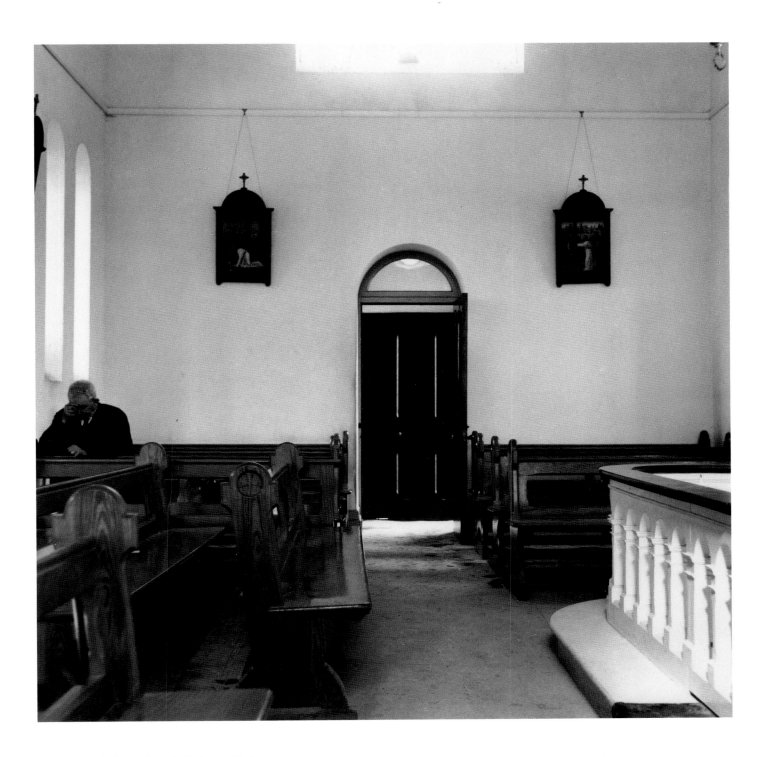

A quiet moment after Mass at Cloonanaha. The Stations of the Cross are copies of the famous Stations at Antwerp Cathedral.

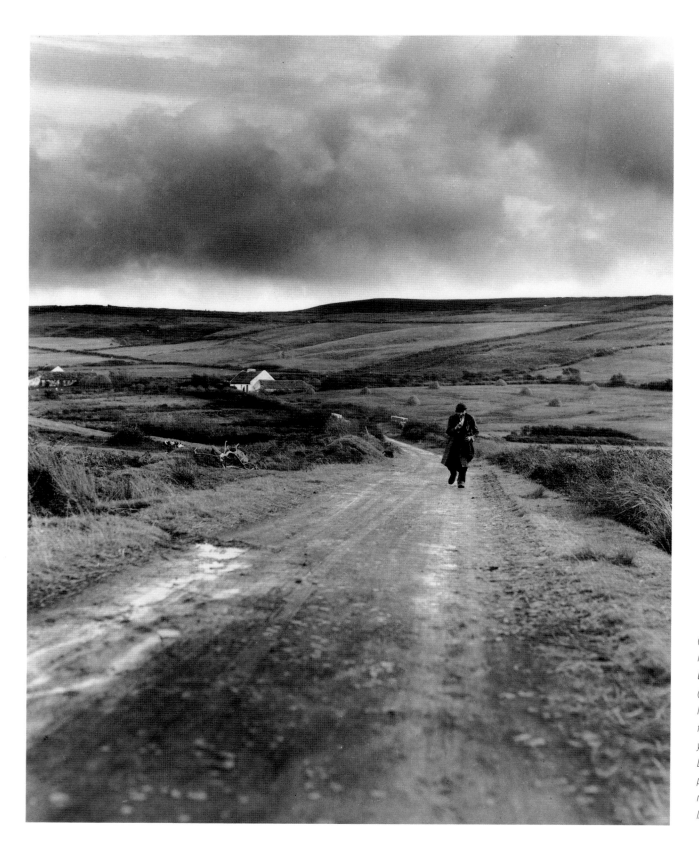

(Left and facing) An old man approaches on a *County Clare* bohereen (small road). "That landscape where the fellow is walking toward you, that's pure Ireland," Lange remarked of this photograph. "He was made out of that wet limy soil, made out of it."

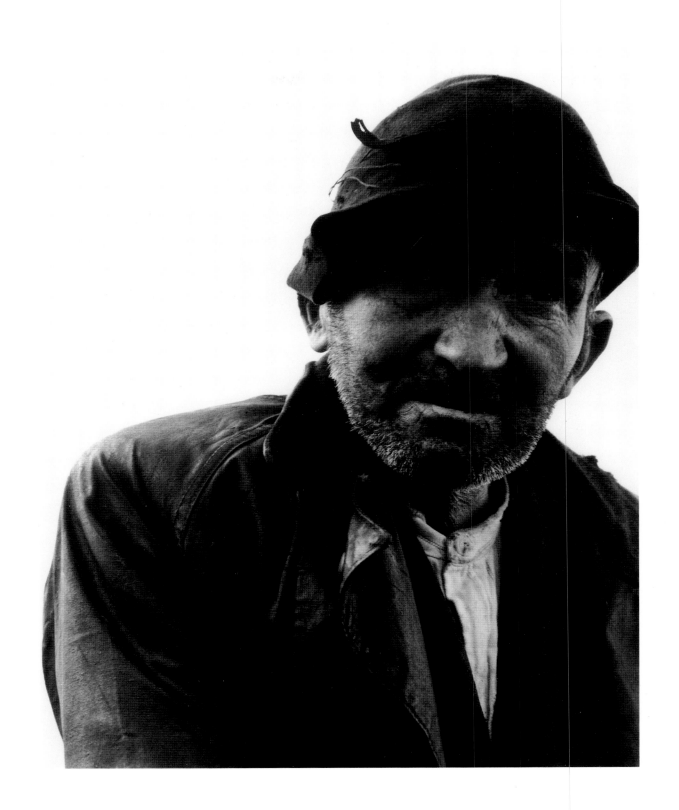

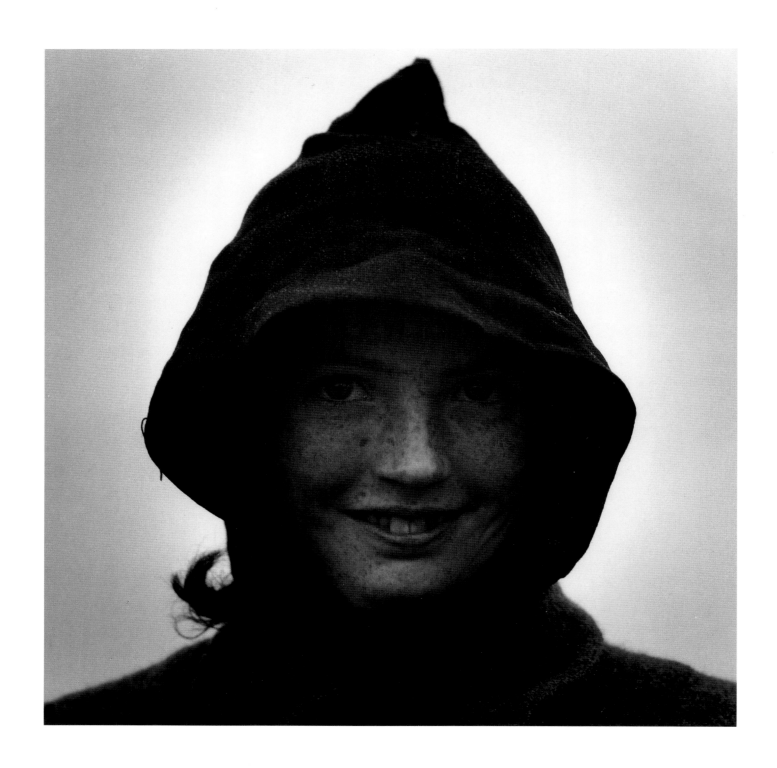

Whenever it rained in Berkeley, Lange hung this picture on her front door to remind her of the rain in Ireland.

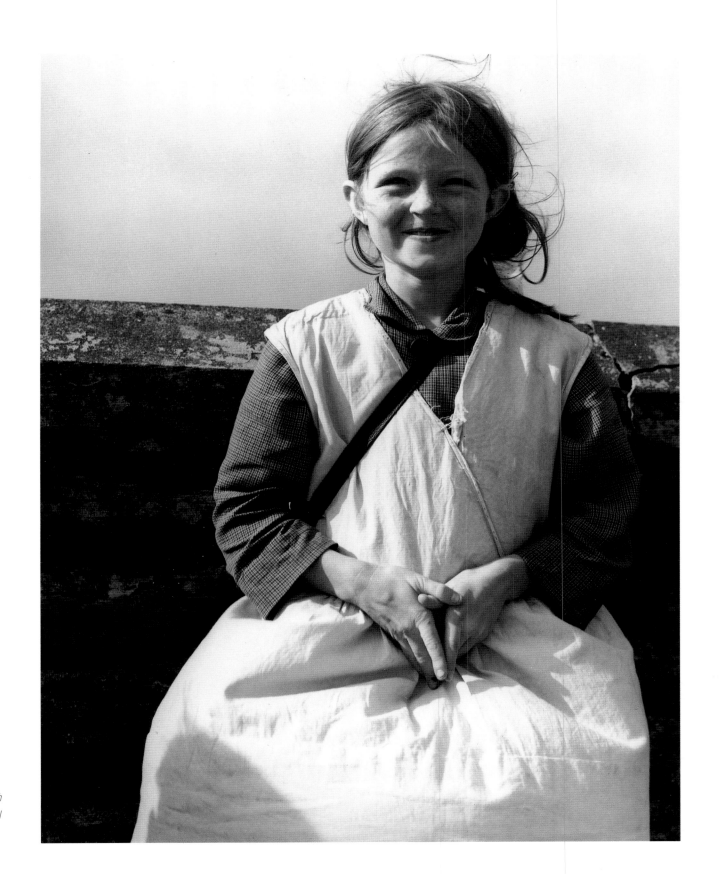

Ten-year-old Bridie O'Halloran speaks Irish and English with equal fluency.

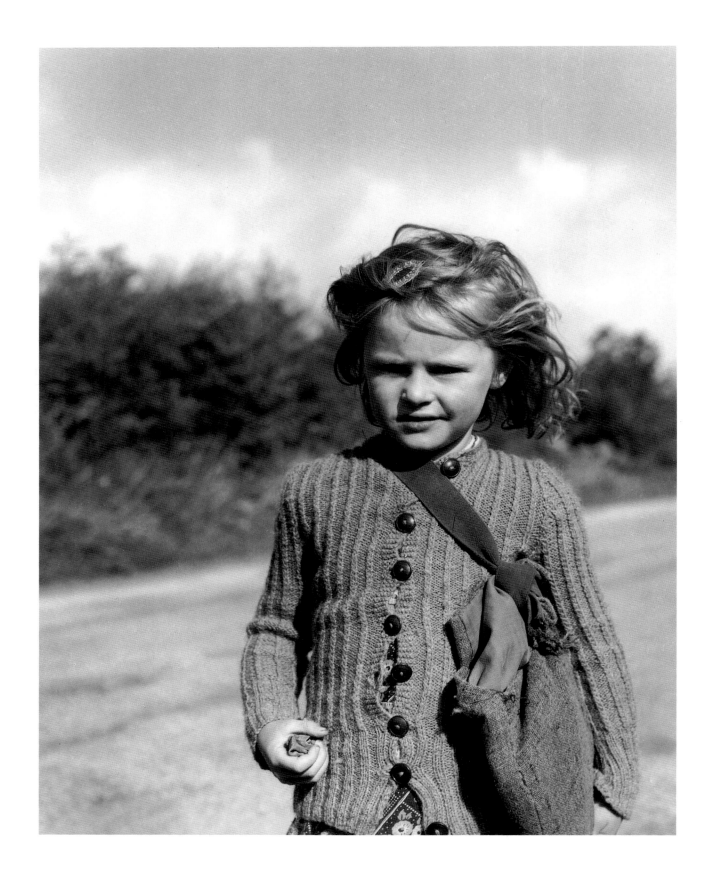

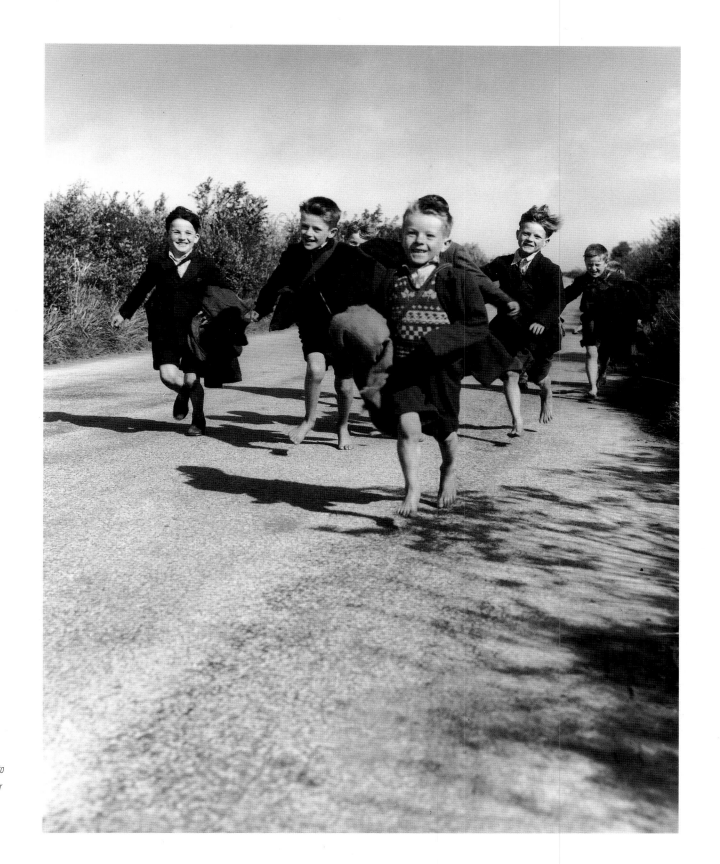

(Right and facing)
Children on their way to
school. During the finer
months, many children
went barefoot.

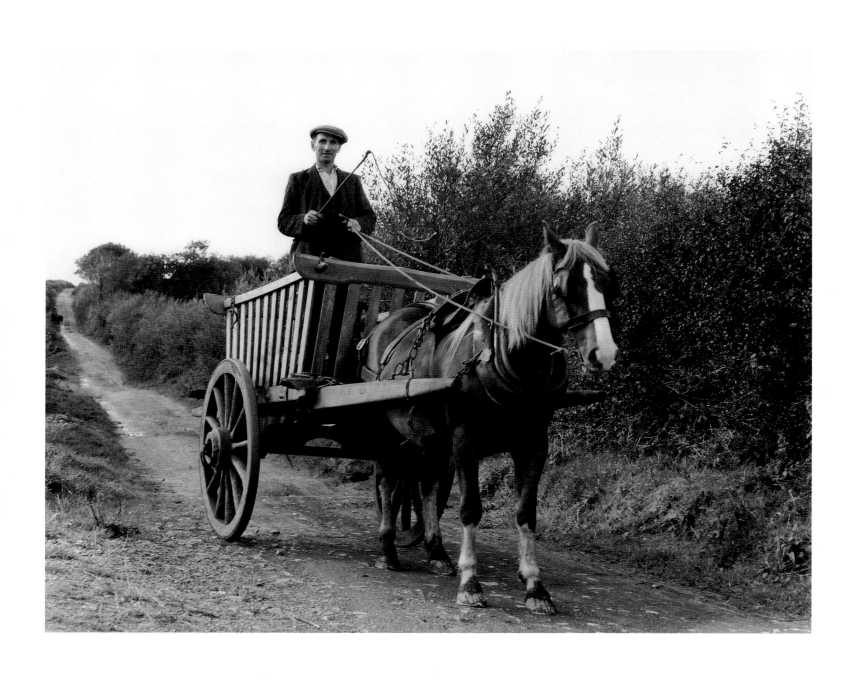

The horse-drawn creel is used for transporting turf, small animals,
and milk containers, as well as people.

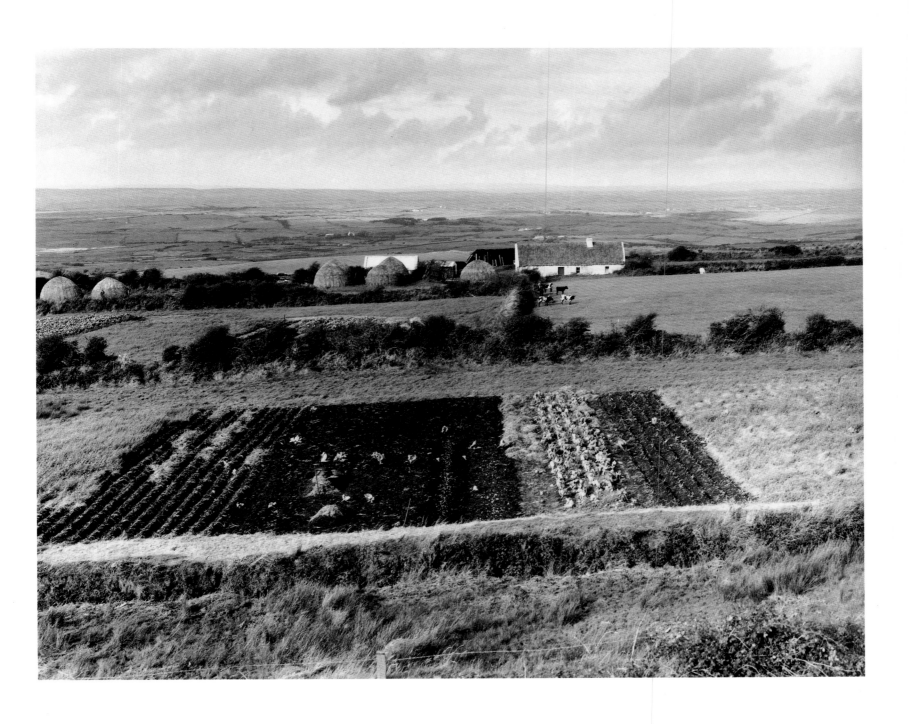

The garden in the foreground provides the farm family with vegetables. The large haycocks near the house provide winter feed for sheep and cattle.

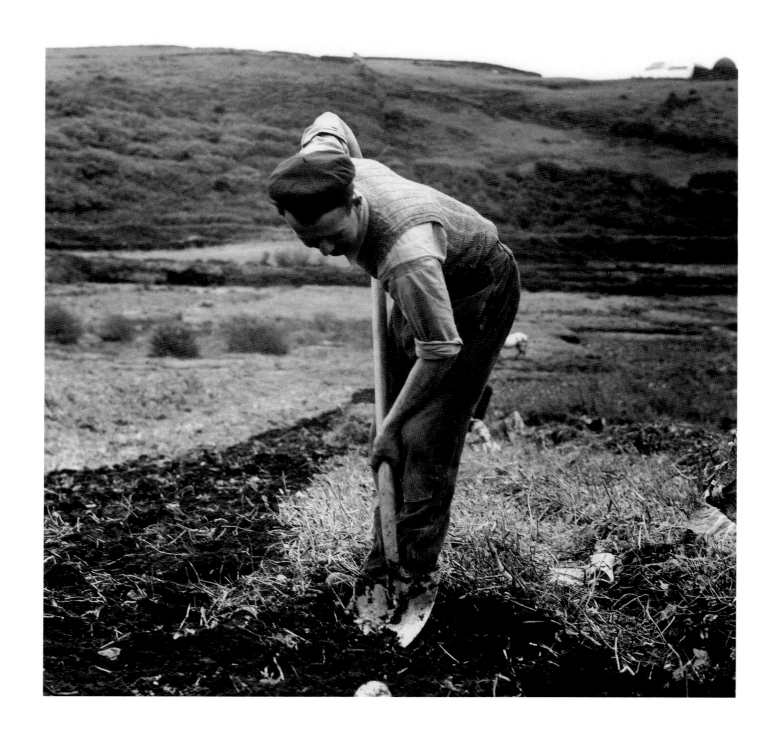

(Above and facing) A man digs potatoes at a farm in Bartra, near Lahinch.

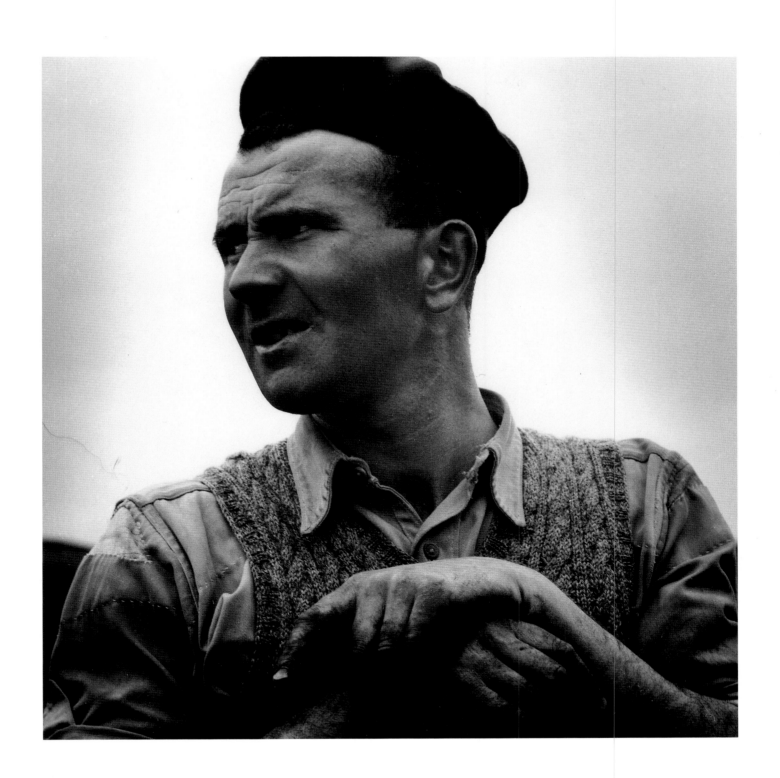

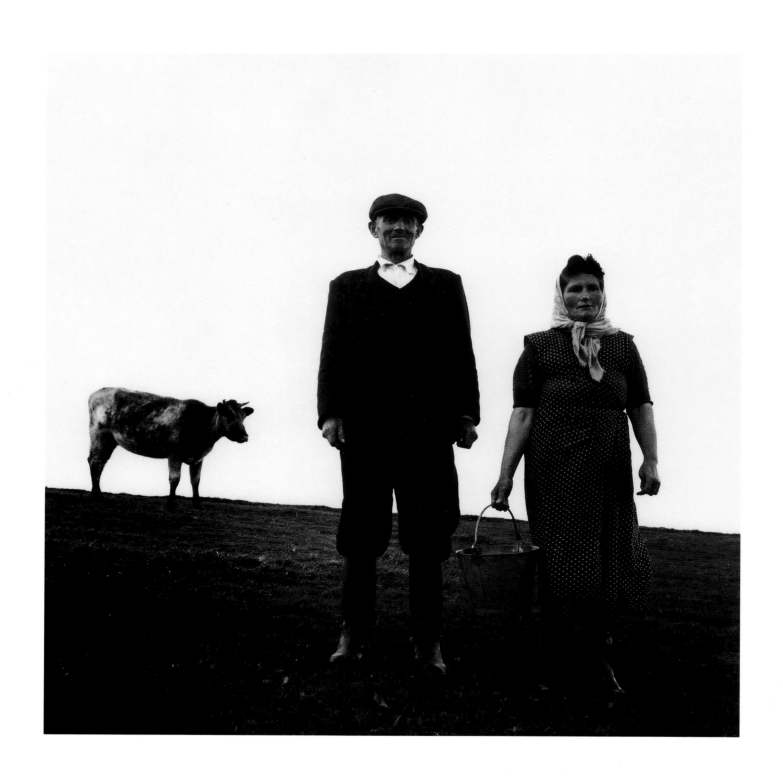

John and Annie O'Halloran prepare to milk cows together on their farm at Mount Callan.

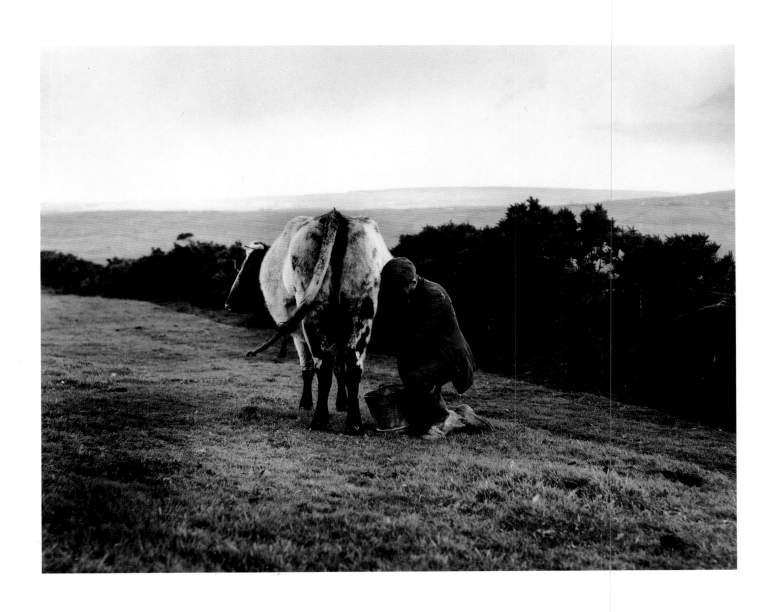

Only a quiet cow can be milked in a field, where she is more likely to kick over the bucket or her owner. John O'Halloran goes about his work without even the use of a stool.

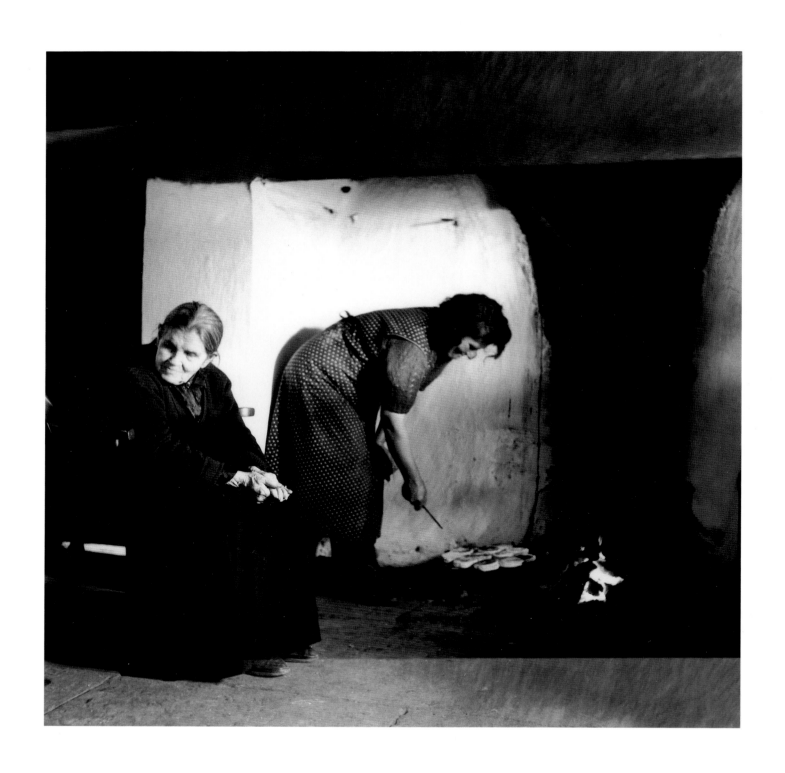

Annie O'Halloran, with her mother-in-law Ellen, prepares potato cakes at their turf fire.

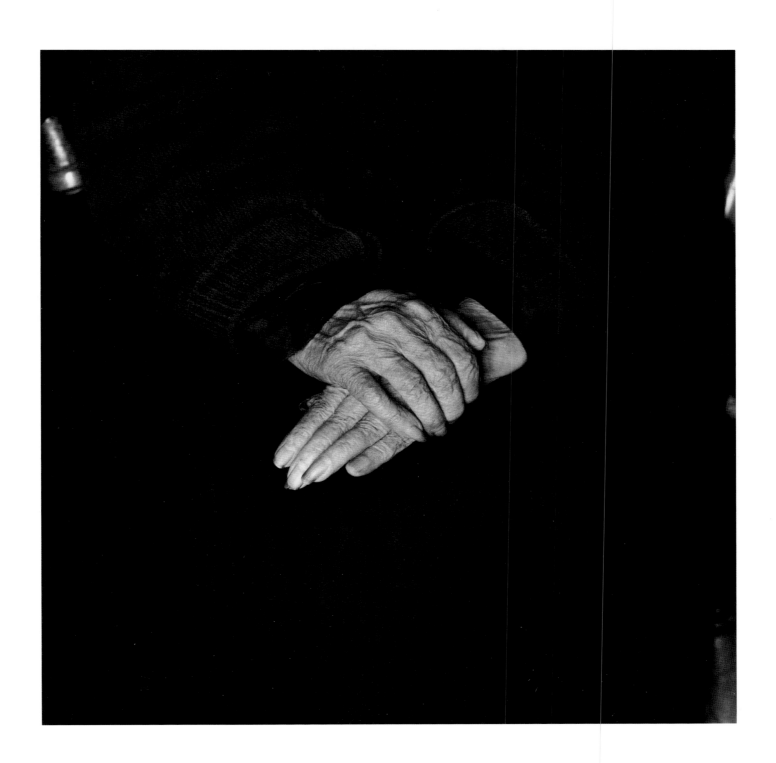

The hands of Ellen O'Halloran, born in 1871.

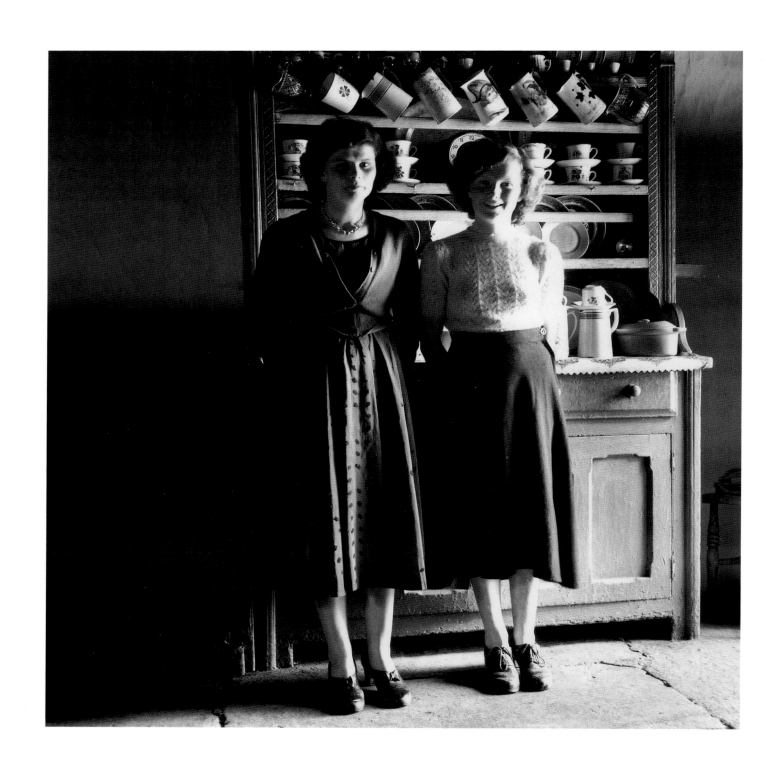

Catherine and Anne O'Halloran.

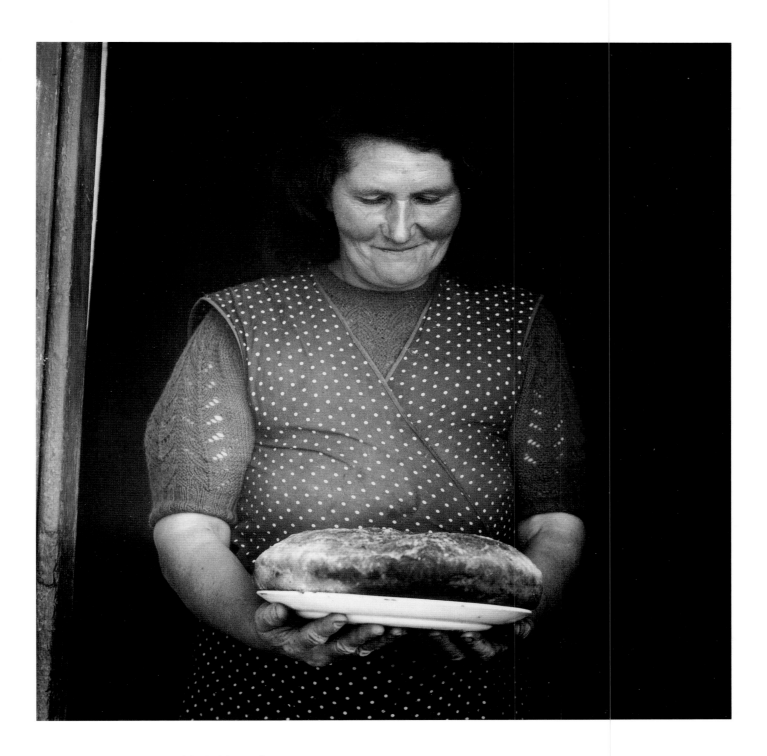

Annie O'Halloran holds the fresh soda bread that she bakes every few days using flour, buttermilk, and baking soda.

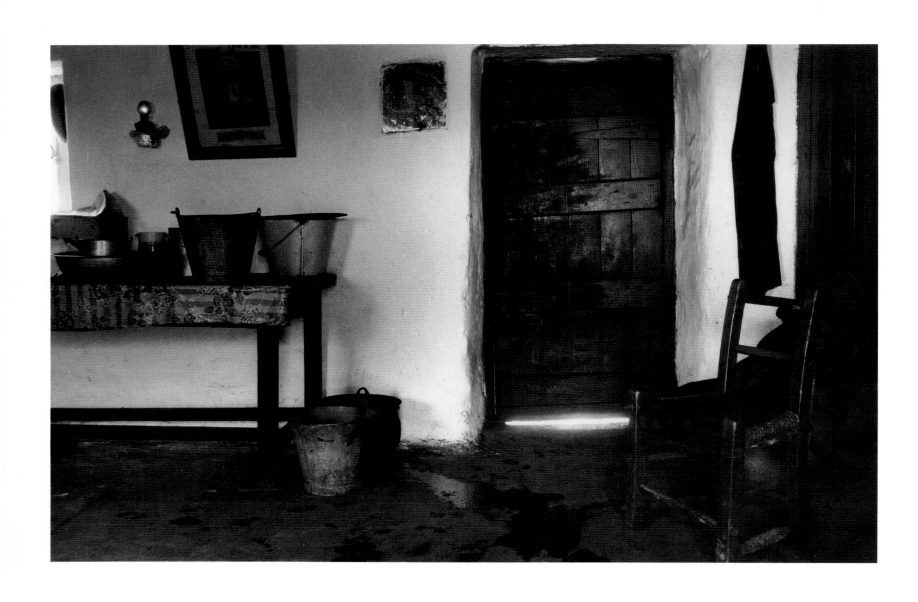

This scene was common in many Irish rural homes. Water drawn from the well is stored in buckets for use by the family during the evening. The picture of the Sacred Heart is always displayed with a small lamp nearby.

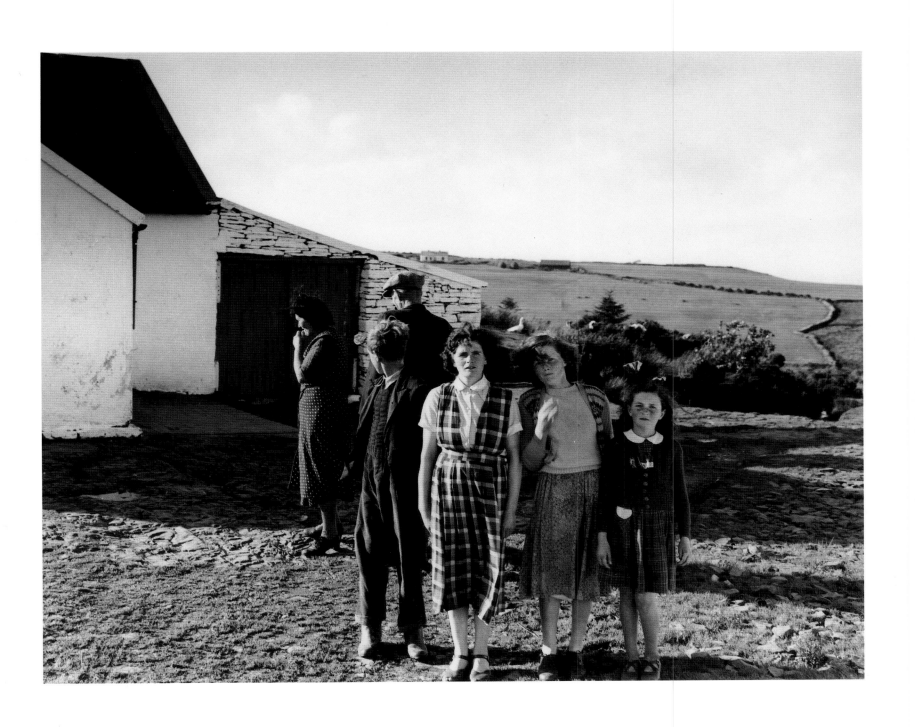

Members of the O'Halloran family of Mount Callan: Annie, John, Séan, Maureen, Anne, and Bernadette. The oldest son Thomas (not pictured) still lives in this house and farms the land.

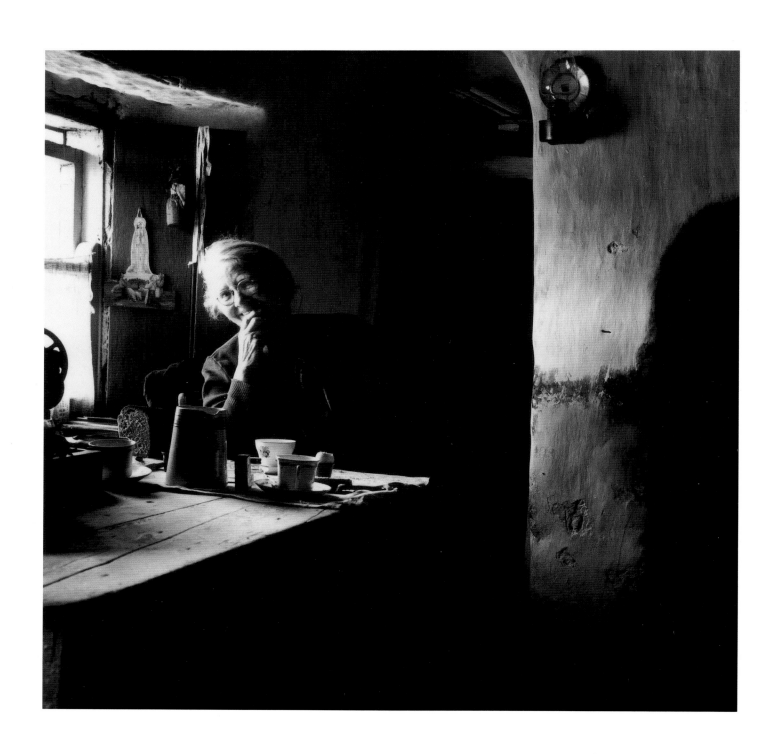

A woman in the kitchen of her house.

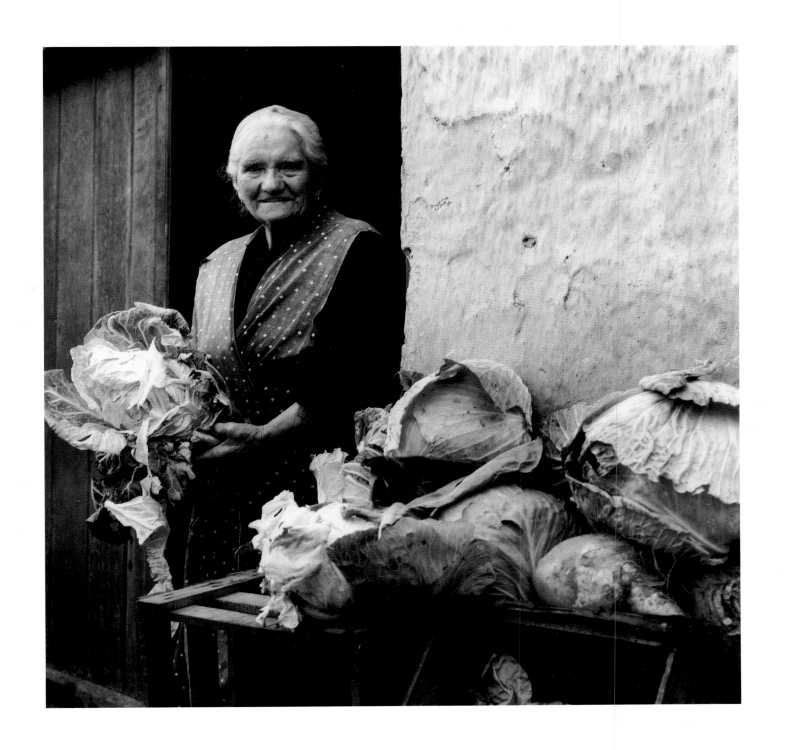

An old woman sells cabbages in Ennis.

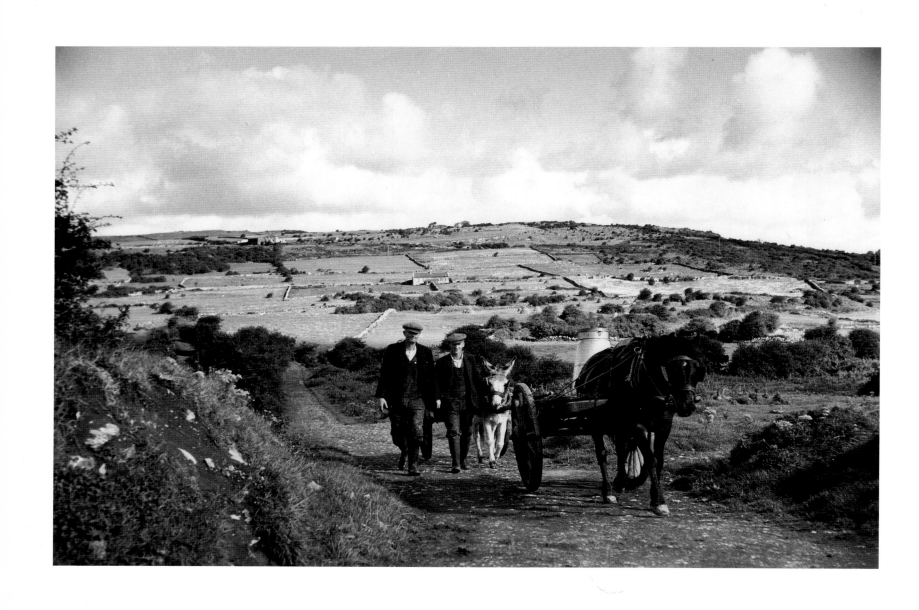

The daily chore of delivering milk to the creamery offers a welcome break from farm work and a chance to catch up on local news. The milk is contained in tall steel drums called churns.

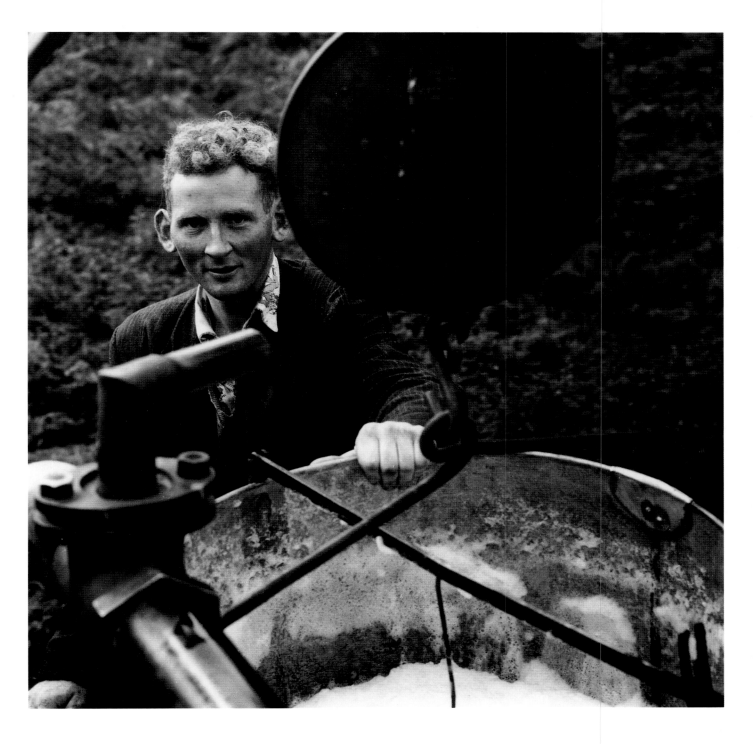

The milk is weighed before it passes through the centrifugal cream separator, which removes the cream from raw milk for use in butter production. The remaining skimmed milk is returned to the farmer, who will feed it to his calves.

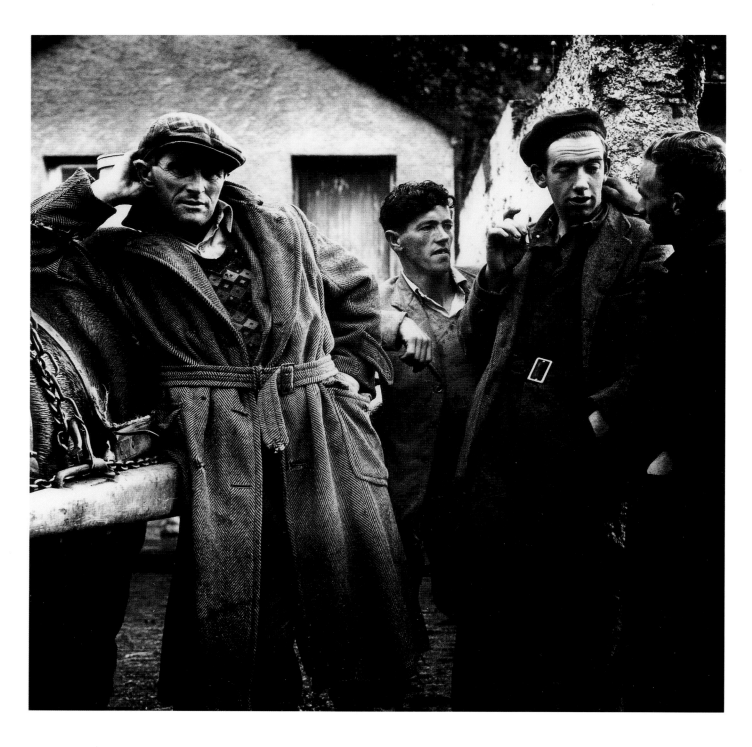

Common in rural districts throughout Ireland, small cooperative creameries have been instrumental in the development of the rural economy. This co-op at Bunratty also provides a good meeting place for farmers waiting their turn to deliver cream.

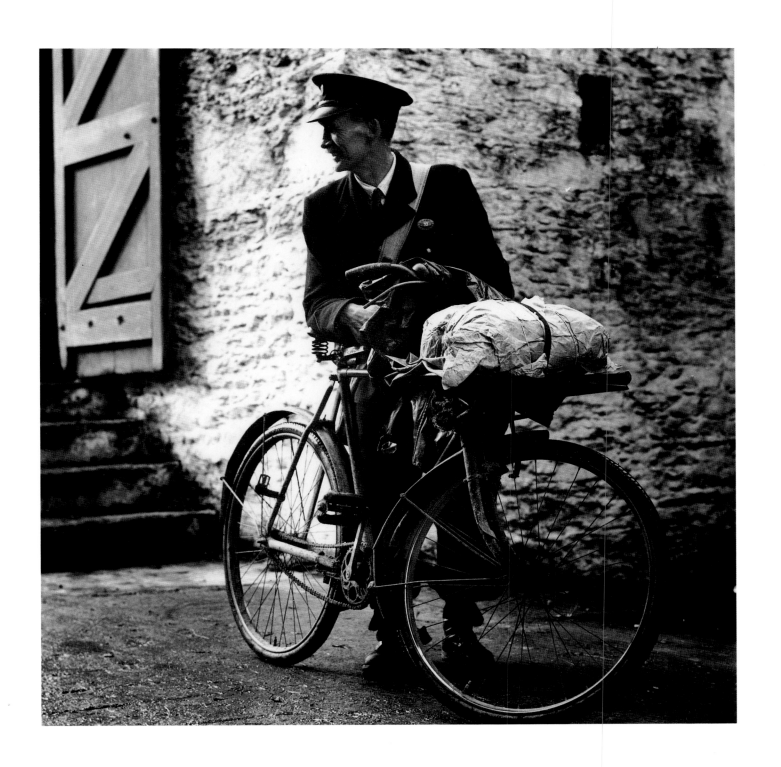

The postman arrives at Bunratty creamery, which was established by local farmers in 1927.

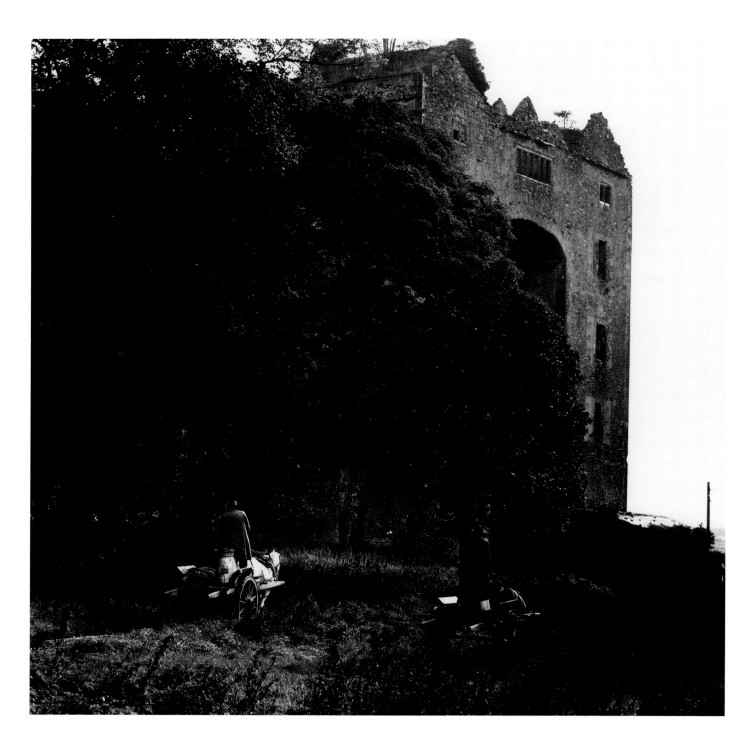

Here, in the shadow of Bunratty Castle, built in 1452 near the River Shannon, countrymen make their way home from Bunratty creamery.

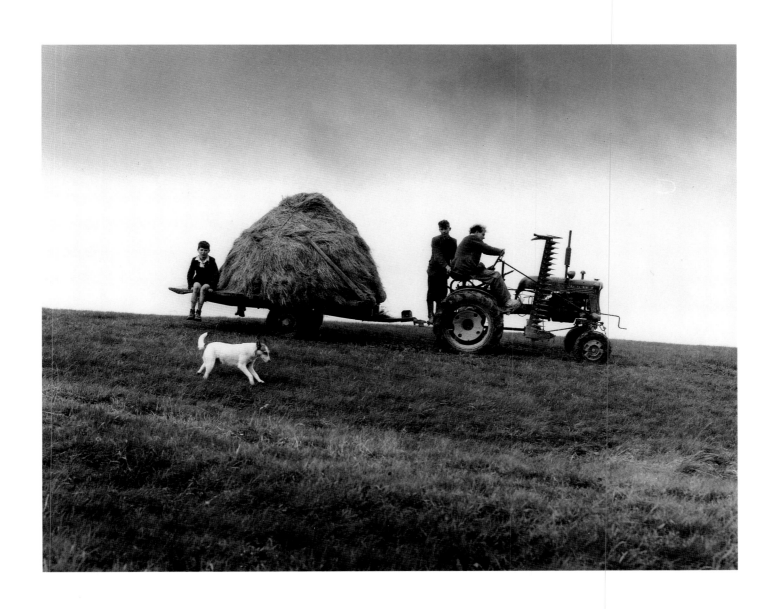

"Saving the hay" is one of the busiest times in the Irish farming calendar. His hayfloat loaded, Robert Tottenham drives his cargo to the haggard *(a small field near the house) with the assistance of two young helpers "lent" by the Woods family nearby. Tractors were seen only on the larger farms in Ireland during the 1950s.*

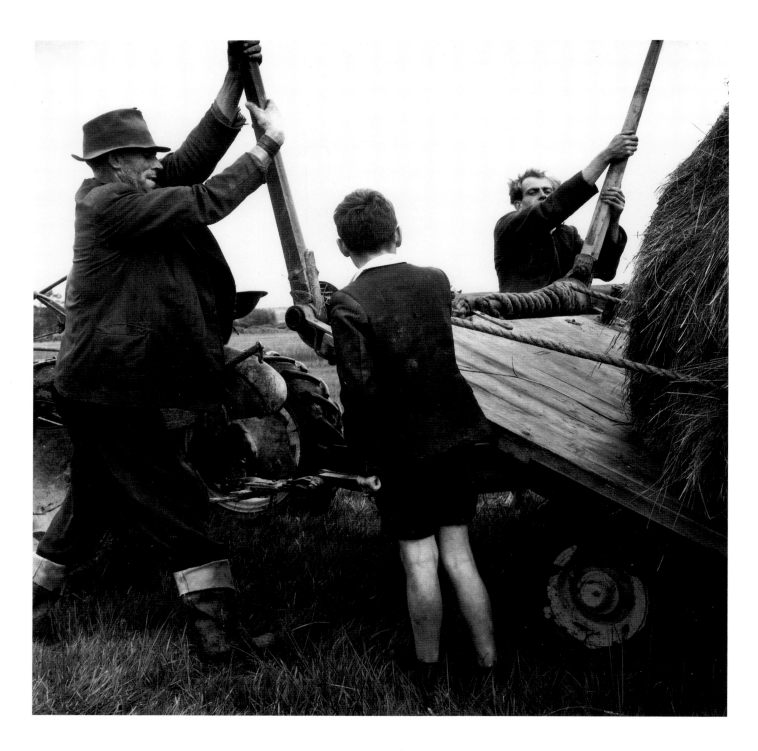

*Gathered in small haycocks about the fields, the cut grass awaits removal by hayfloat
to the hayrick (a large haystack). Pulleys are used to crank the haycocks onto the hayfloat.*

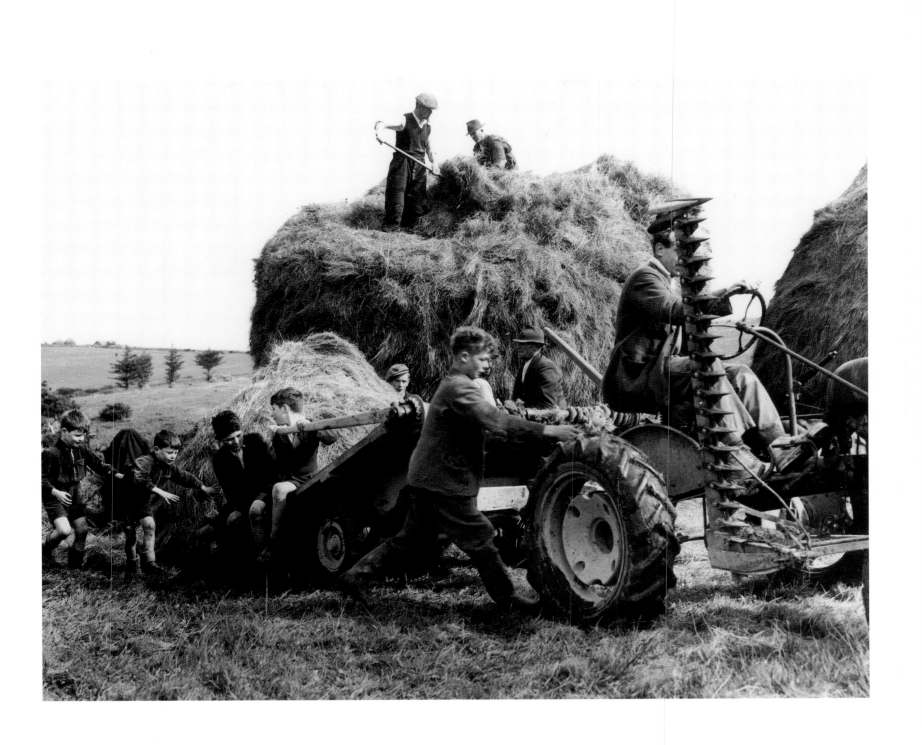

The cut grass is delivered at the hayrick by tipping the hayfloat.

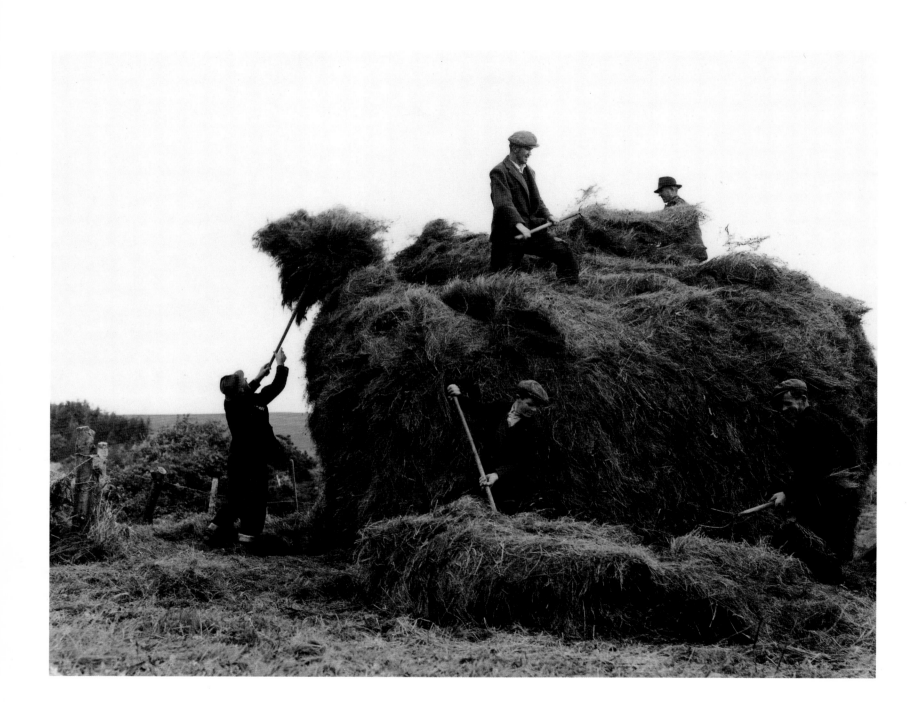

The man at the top of the hayrick is called "the stomper." He distributes the grass carefully to ensure stability and resistance to the elements. The men on the ground are known as "forkers."

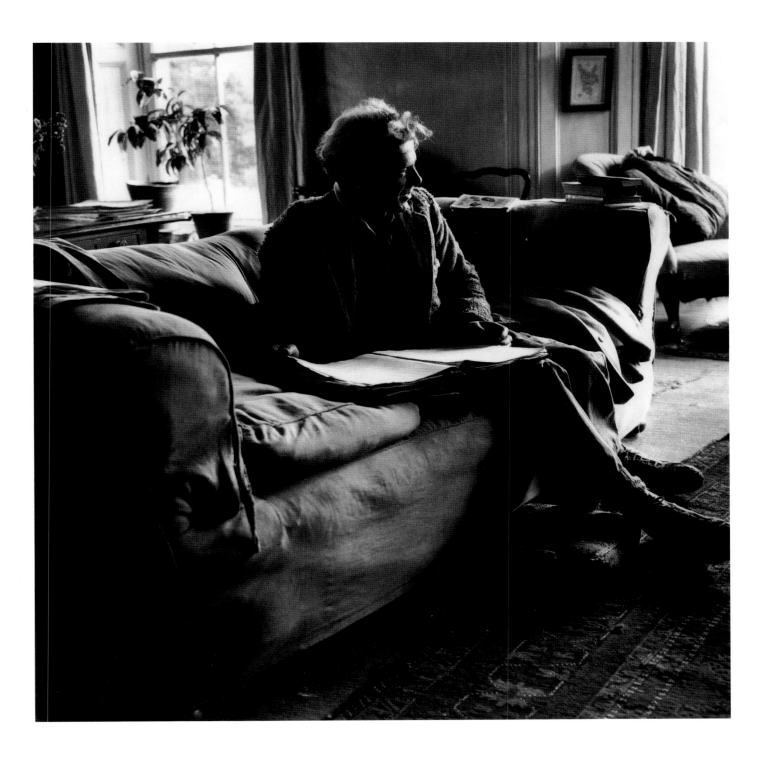

The Tottenham family were absentee landlords on 1,200 acres at Mount Callan beginning in the 1820s, and they built a house there in 1865. Here Robert Tottenham looks over old family documents.

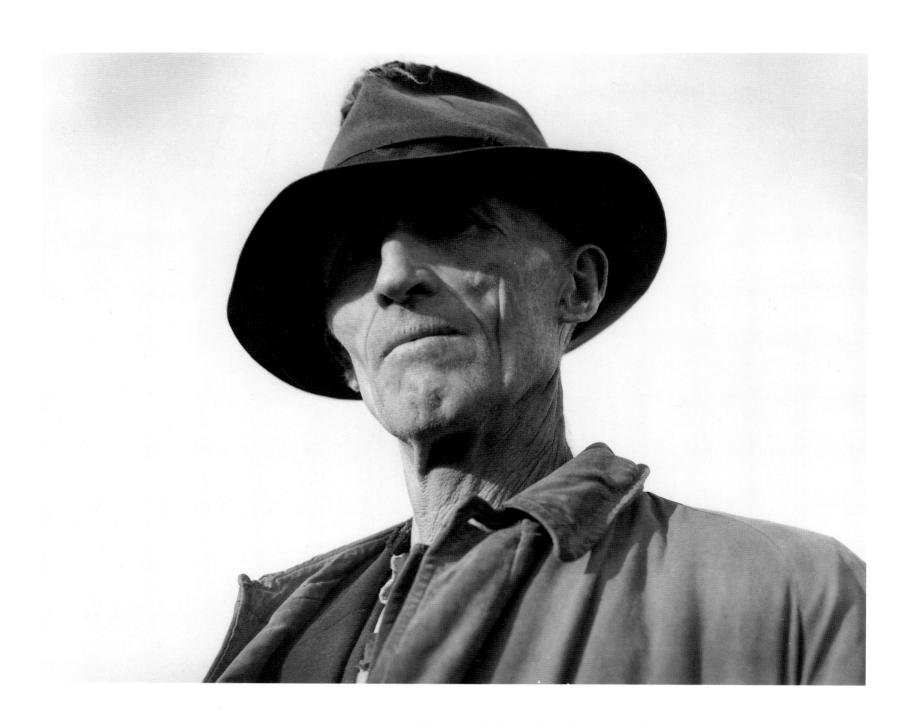

After Lange met this old séanachaí (a storyteller), she noted: "Overlooking his house and acres stands one of the magnificent stone ruins from an ancient past. I asked 'How old might this castle be?' 'Madam, we are much too young to know,' he answered."

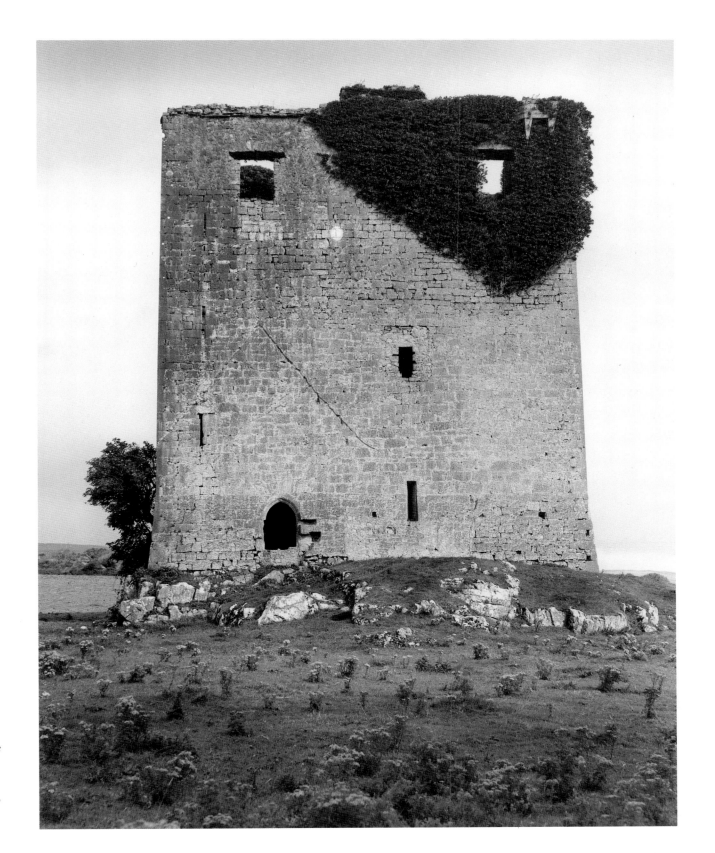

Cratloe Moyle Castle dates back to the early 16th century. Its last occupant was John McNamara, who died in 1780.

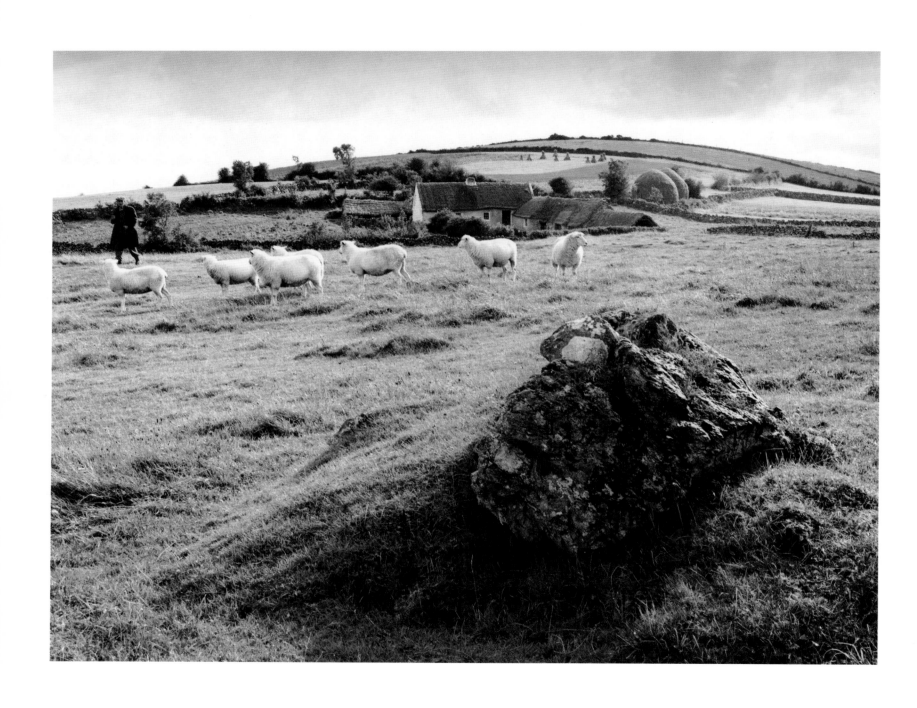

Sheep graze the thin soil that is occasionally breached by hard limestone.

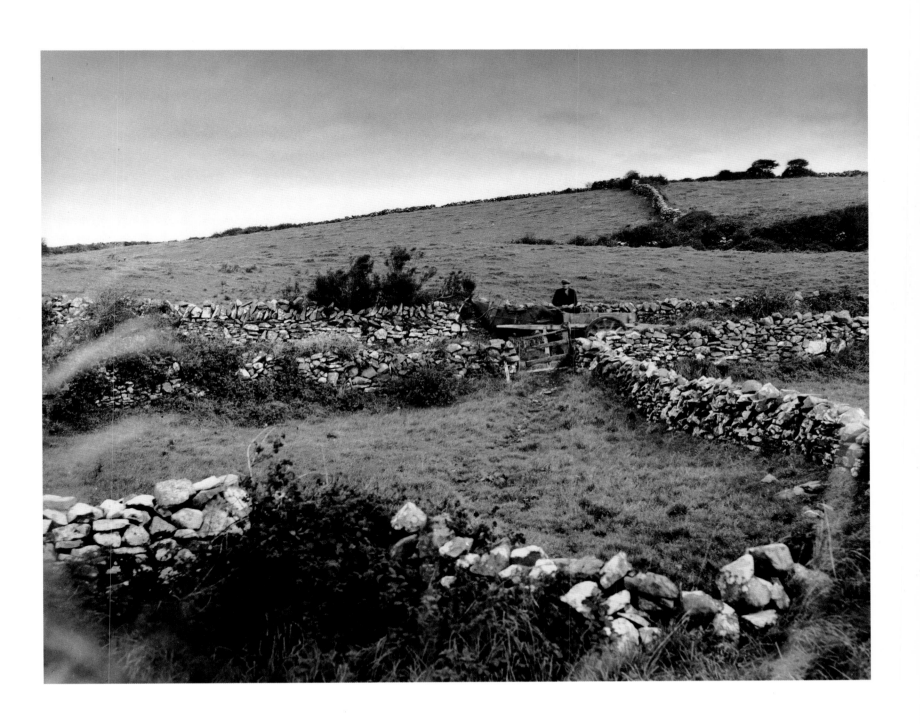

Stone walls and small fields remain symbolic of the Irish western counties.

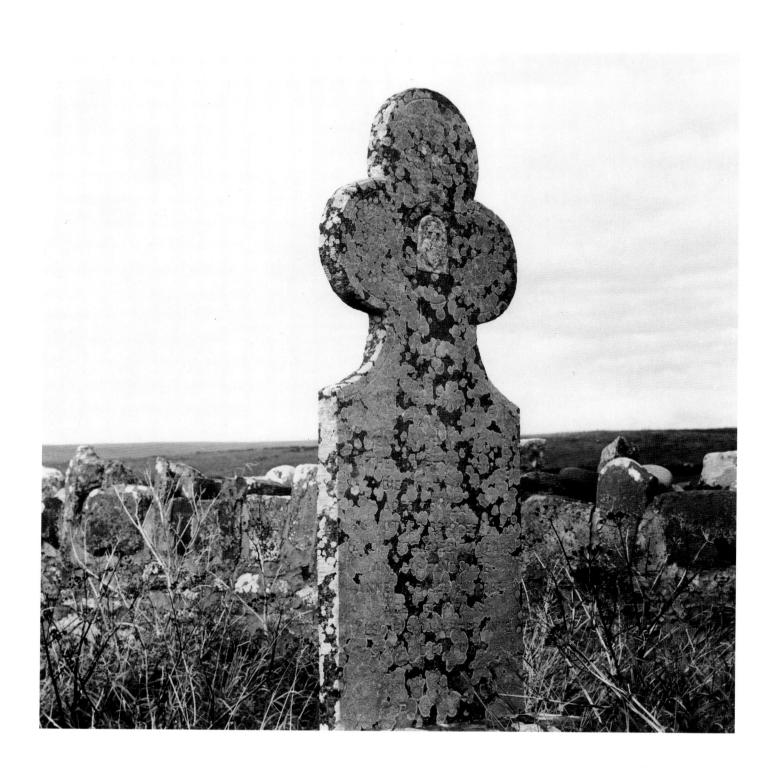

Marking two graves are an old headstone (above), encrusted with lichen, and the less common flatstone (facing).

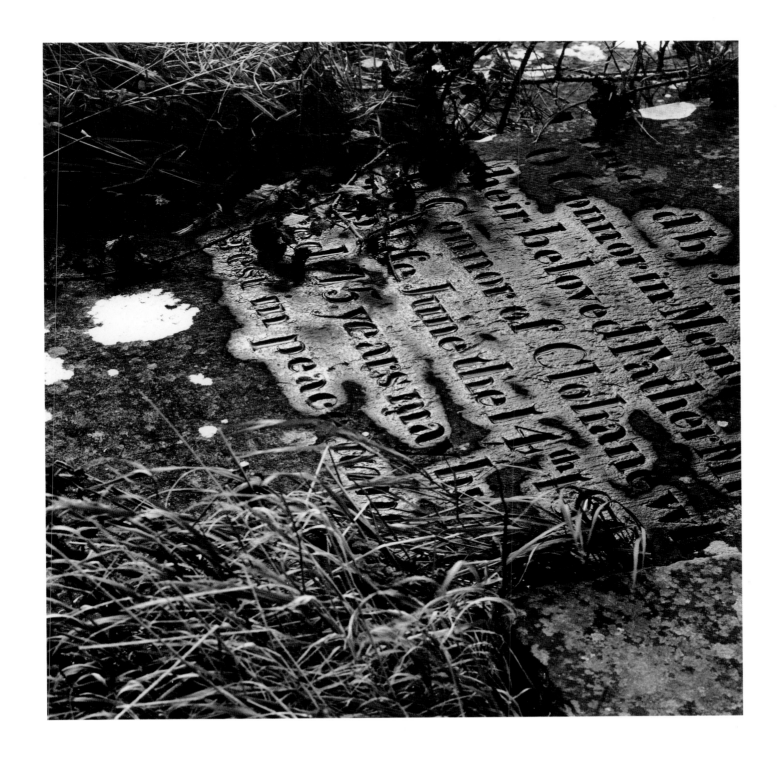

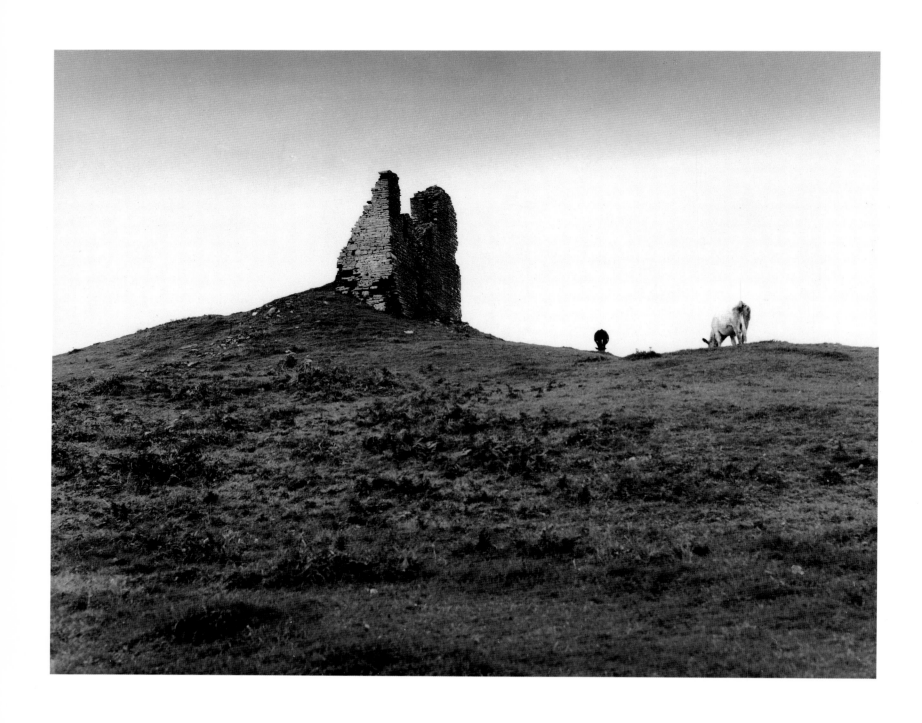

Near Ennistymon, cattle graze around what is left of Glan Castle.

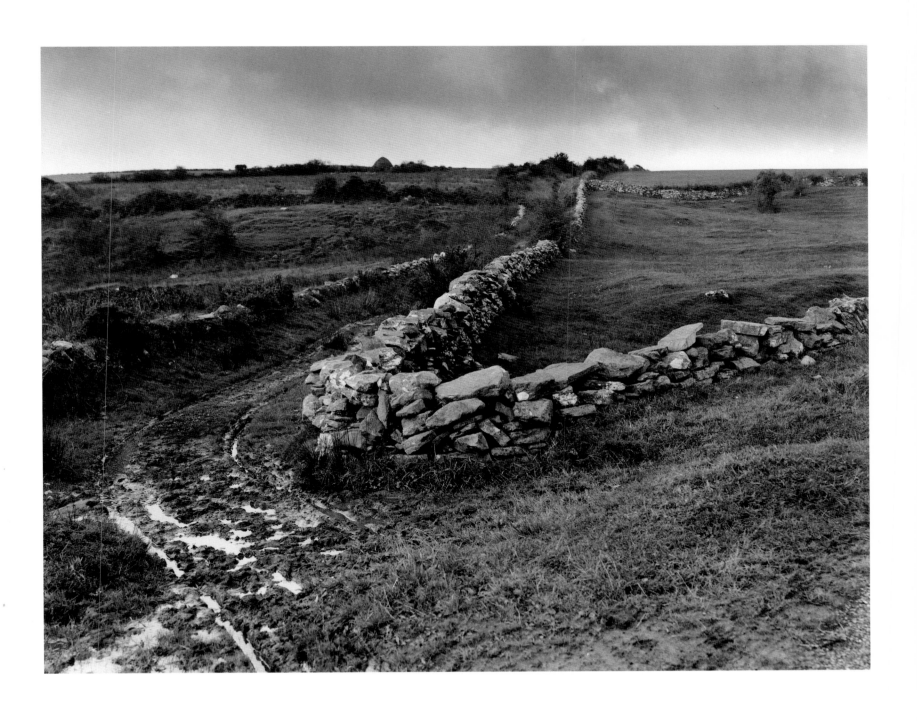

A wet lane in County Clare offers just a taste of the flooding expected before winter ends.

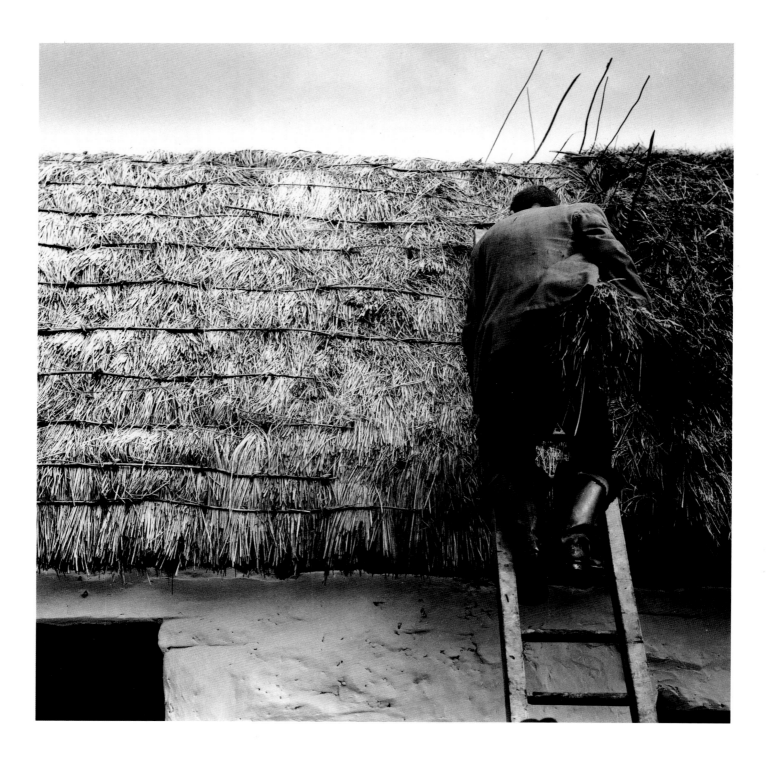

Irish roofs were traditionally thatched with scollops, or sally rods, pinning down the thatch. If the work is well-finished, the rods will be hidden, for exposed rods tend to let water seep through the straw.

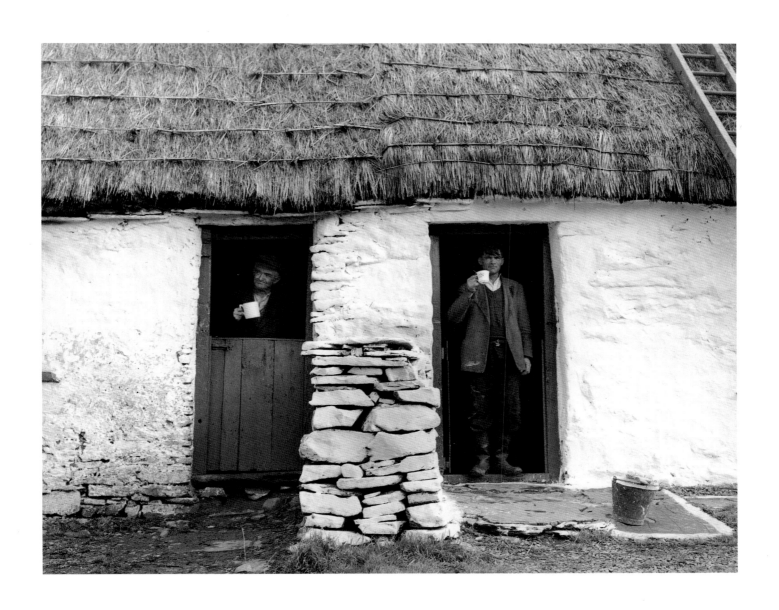

Jimmy Tobin and John Bane drink tea as they rest from thatching their adjoining homes at the edge of Ennistymon.

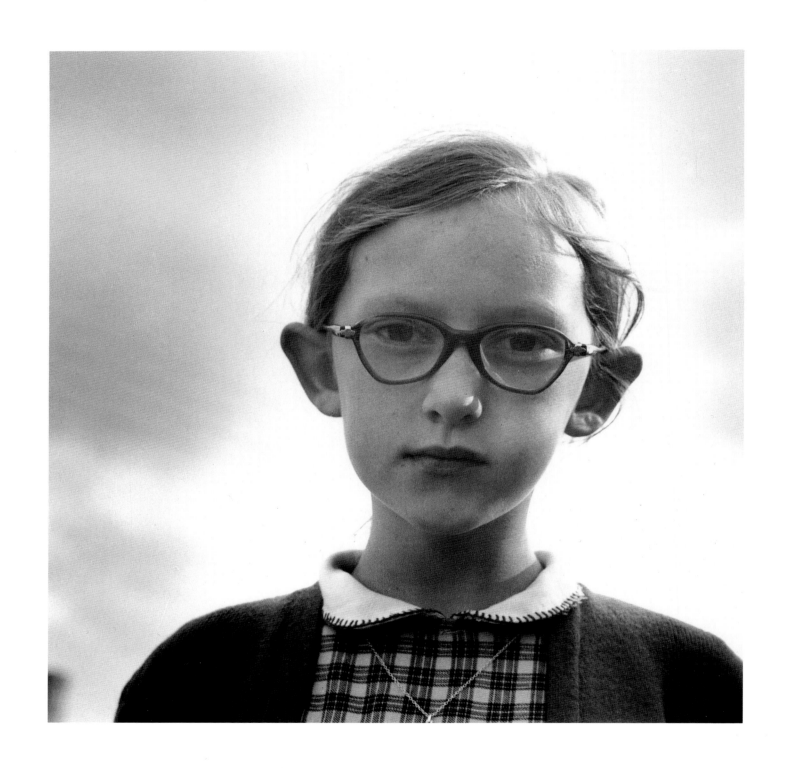

A young girl in Ennis.

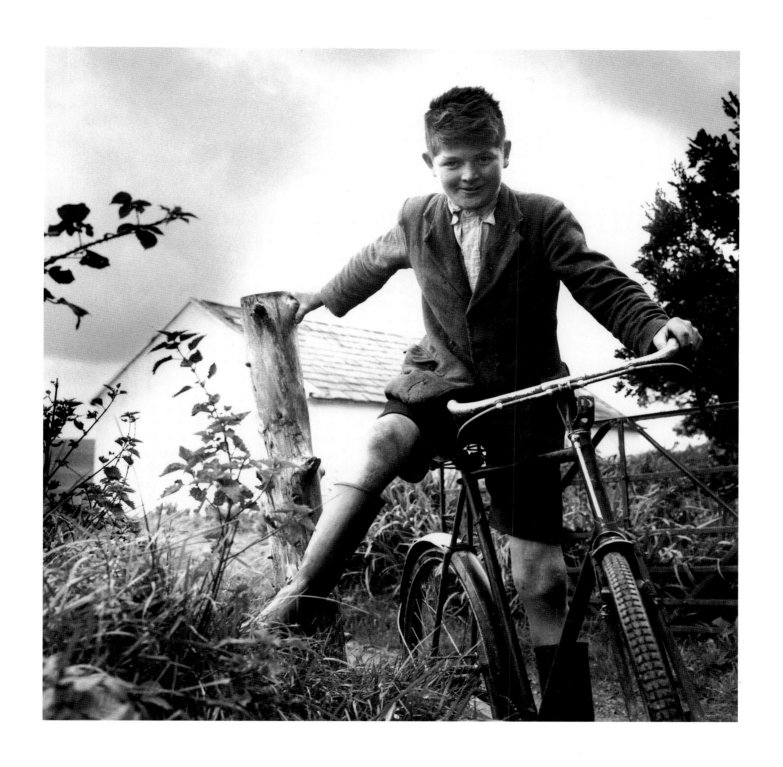

A boy on his bike, a common mode of transportation at this time.

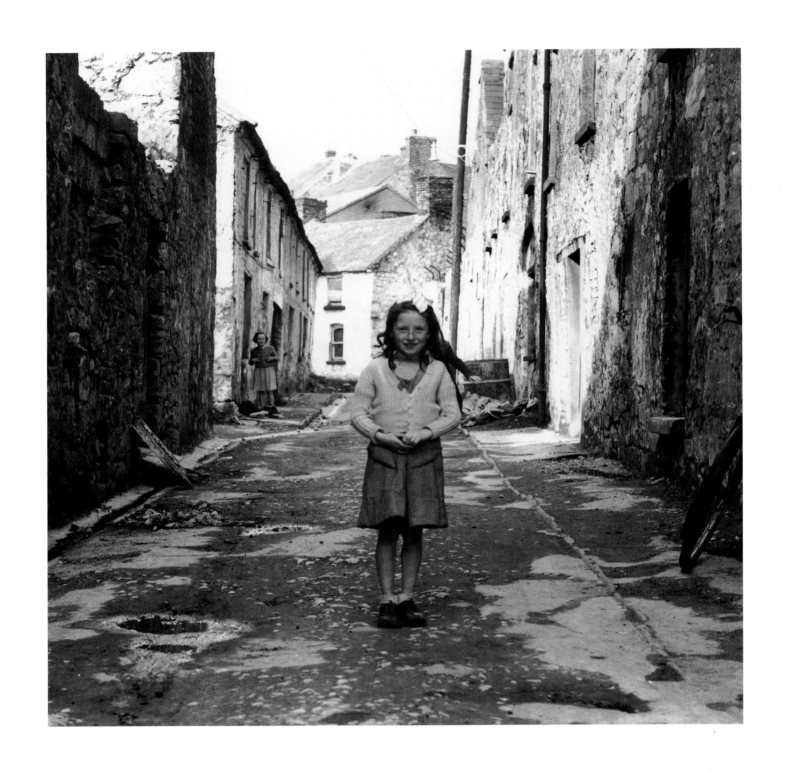

A girl stands in an Ennis lane near the Old Ground Hotel.

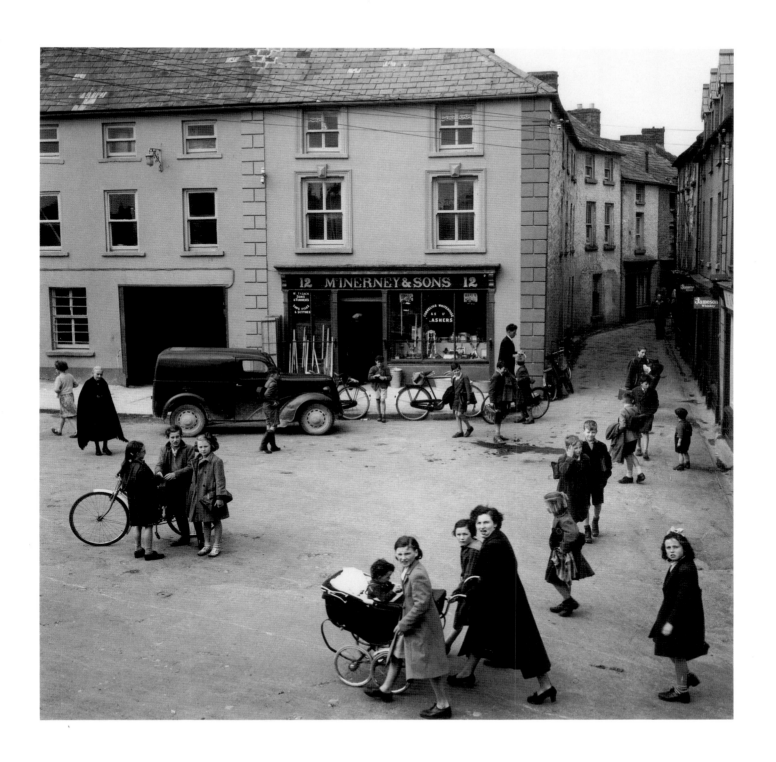

Lower Market Street, Ennis, taken from Dennis Wylde's photographic studio.

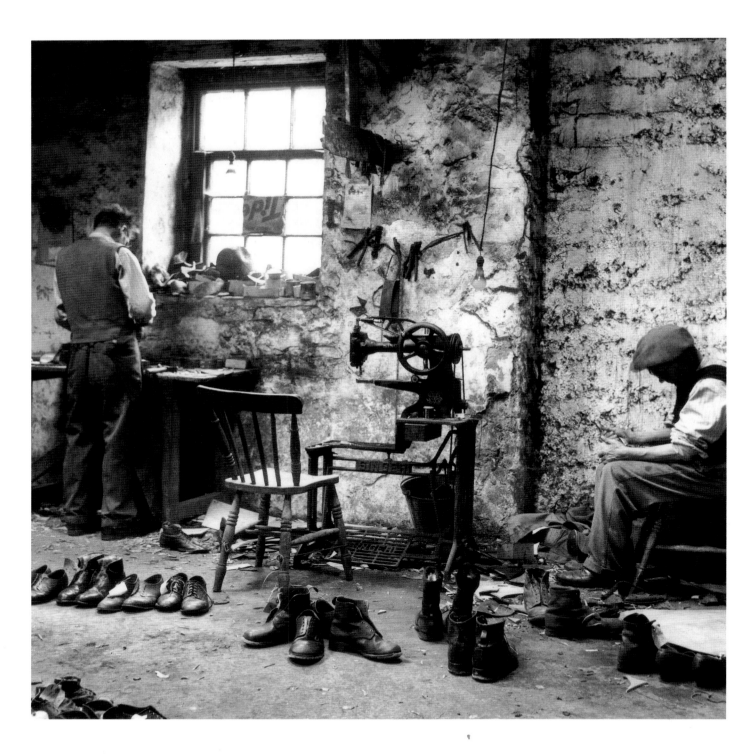

Michael Kelly (at right) has repaired shoes all his life. He works for James "The Yank" Kelly (no relation), a local who once lived in New Hampshire and was said to have returned to Ireland with a dreadful accent. Although "The Yank" cannot read or write, his business employs five other men.

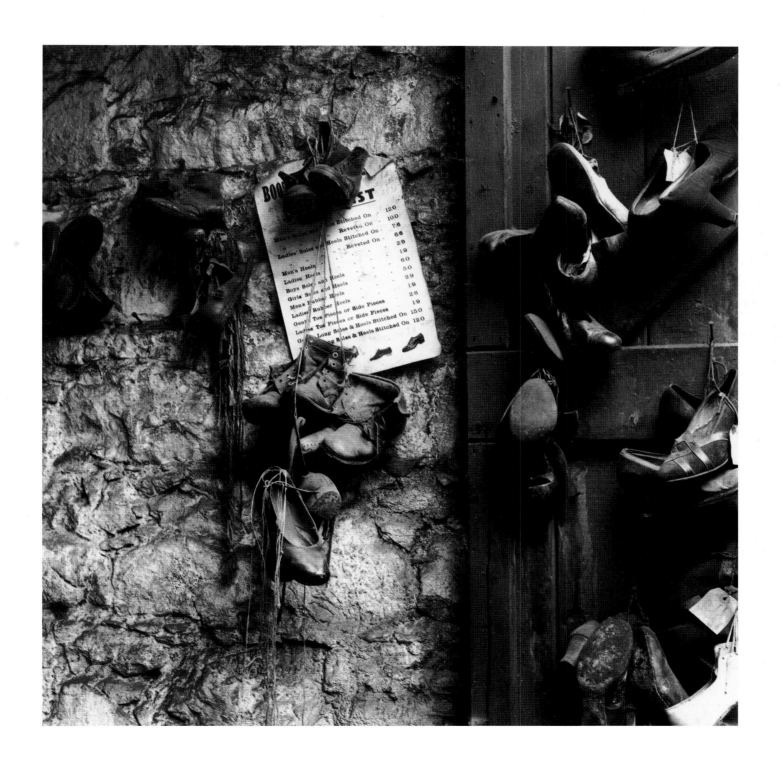

The price list hangs among repaired shoes at James Kelly's cobbler business in Ennis.

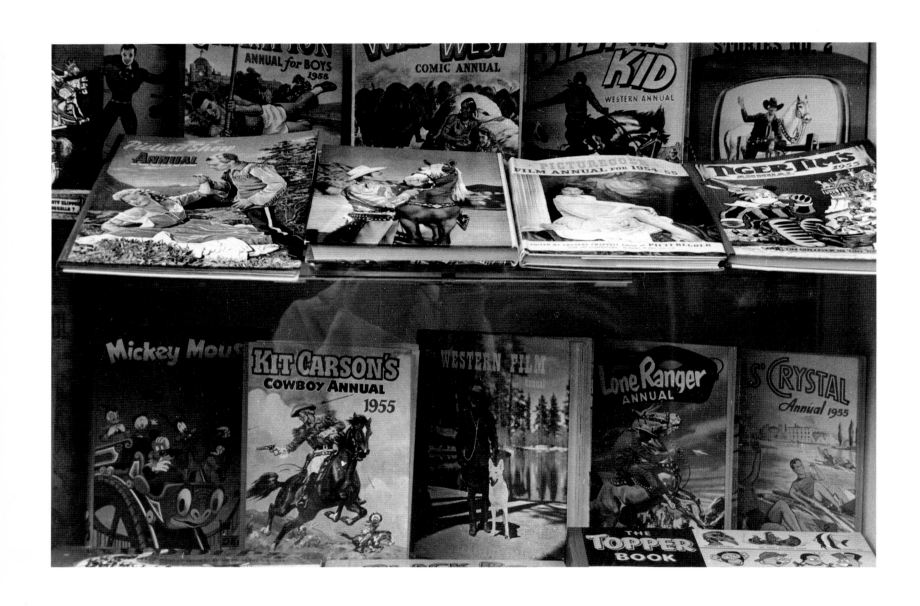

A Dublin shop window shows the selection of comic books available to young readers. Most of the material is American in origin and based on popular movie heroes of the day.

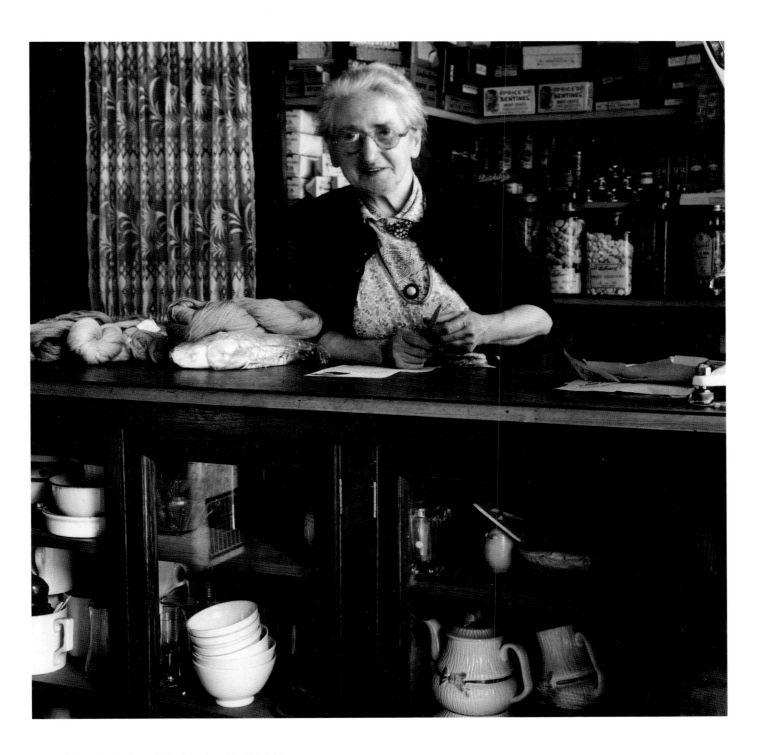

Bridget Wylde tends to her shop on Market Street, Ennis. Mrs. Wylde's living area
is behind the curtain on the left.

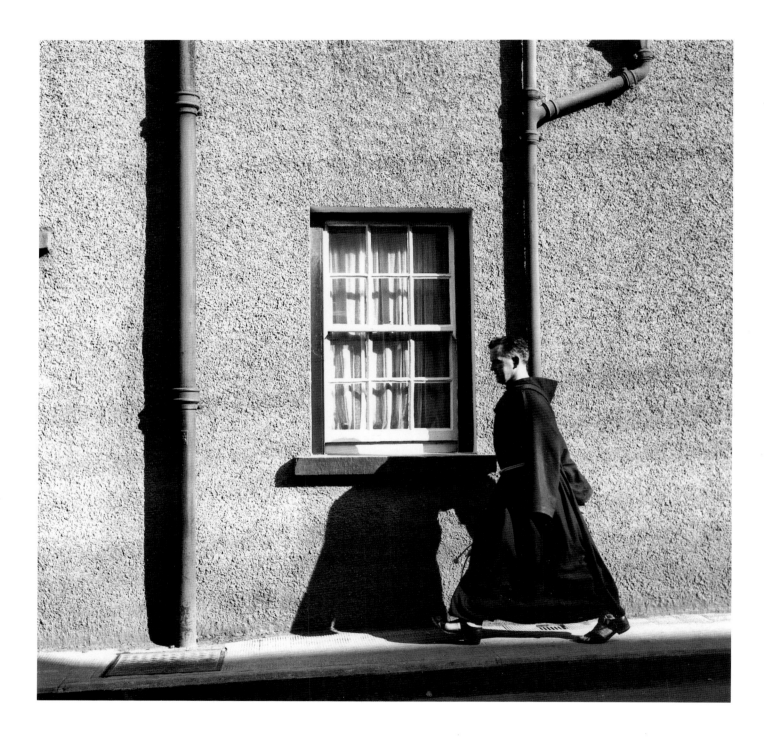

Father Carthage, a Franciscan friar from the local St. Flannan's School, strides beside the Old Ground Hotel. Save for a brief disappearance from the town during the occupation of Oliver Cromwell, the Franciscans have been in Ennis for more than 750 years.

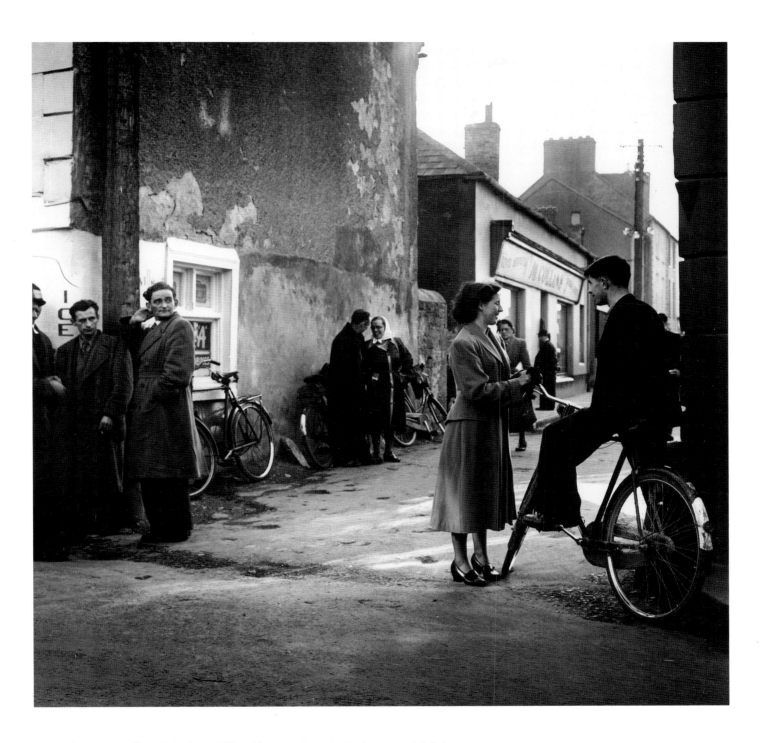

A couple chat at the corner of Lower Market Street and O'Connell Street, a regular meeting place for young people in Ennis.
The town's only picture house, The Gaiety, is across the street and is probably the reason that people are gathered here.

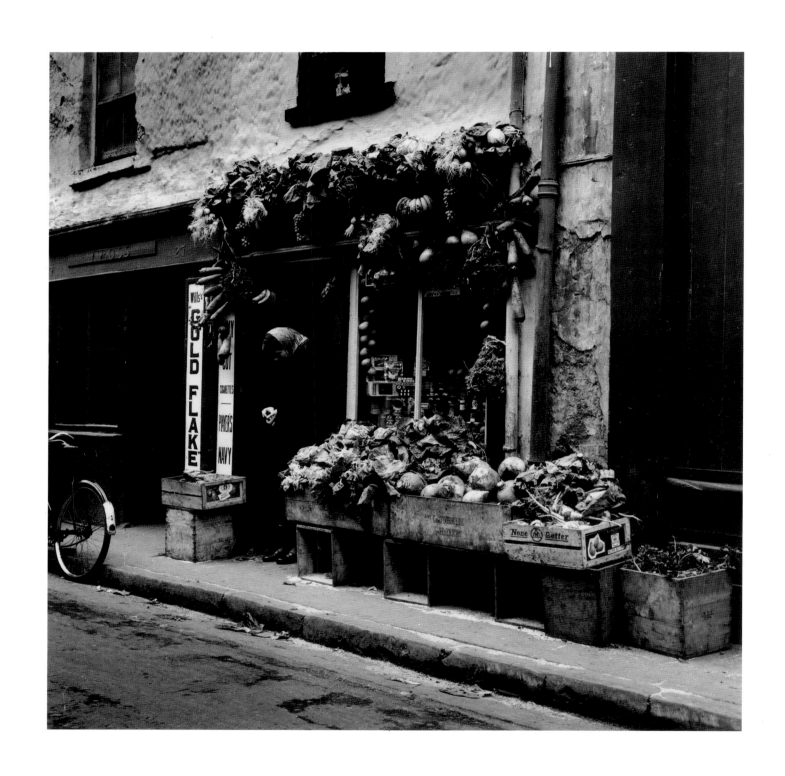

Clem Ryan's fruit and vegetable shop on Parnell Street, Ennis.

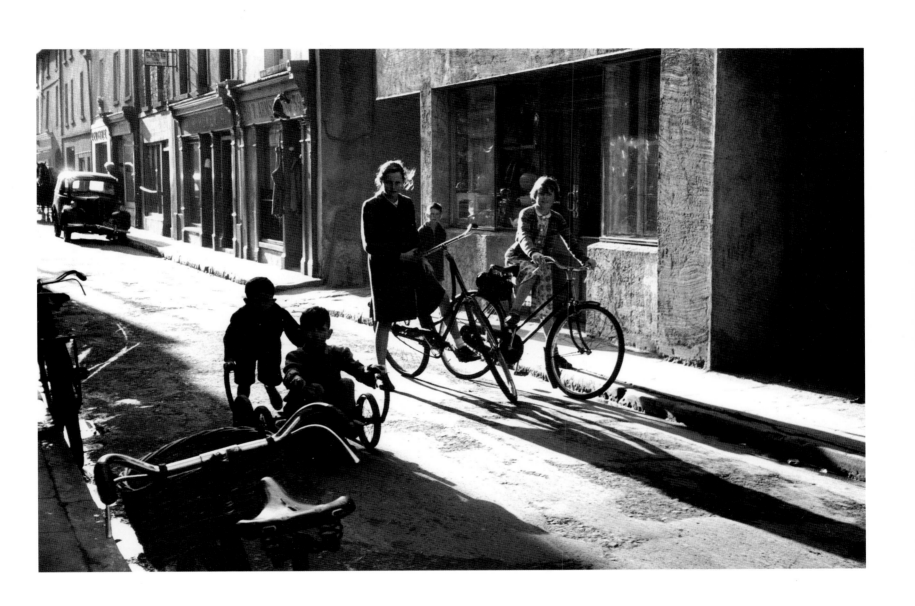

Two boys play with pram wheels on Parnell Street, Ennis.

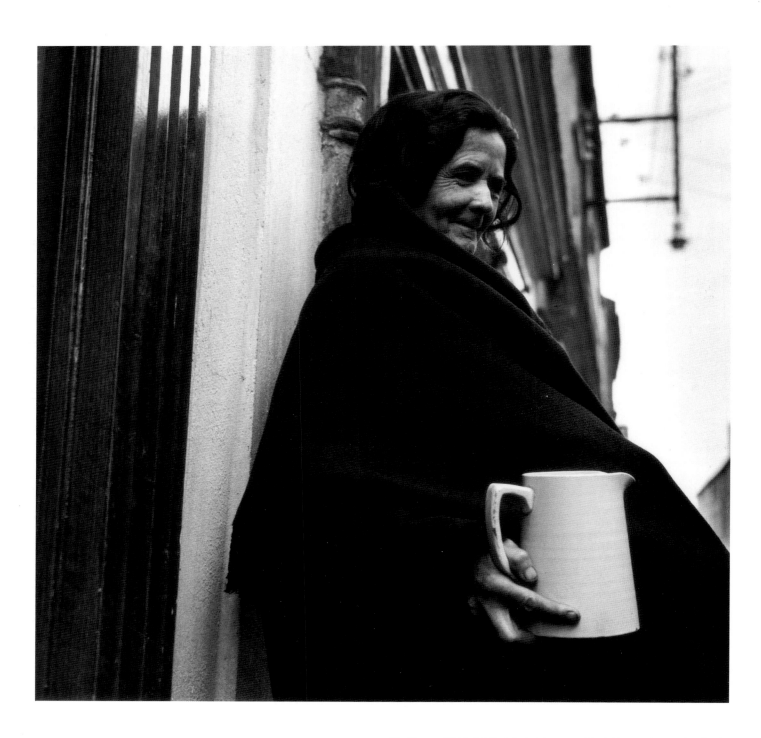

Ellen Shannon of Old Market Street, Ennis, is known as a "shawlie" because she wraps herself in the thick black shawl symbolic of widowhood. Here she holds her jug of milk while pausing for a chat.

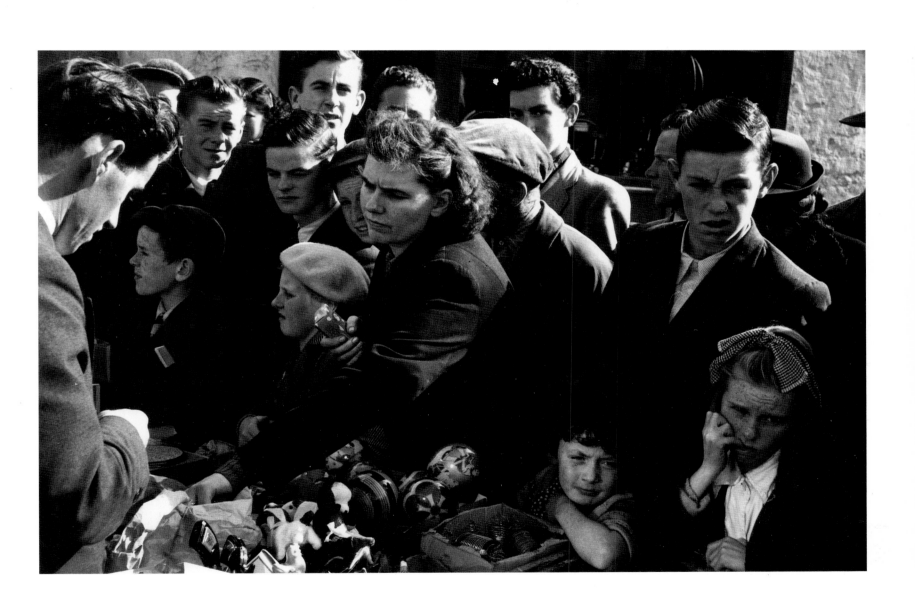

The Ennis market has been held on Friday evenings and Saturday mornings for 300 years.
A good place to buy vegetables or toys, it is also popular among those who just like to browse.

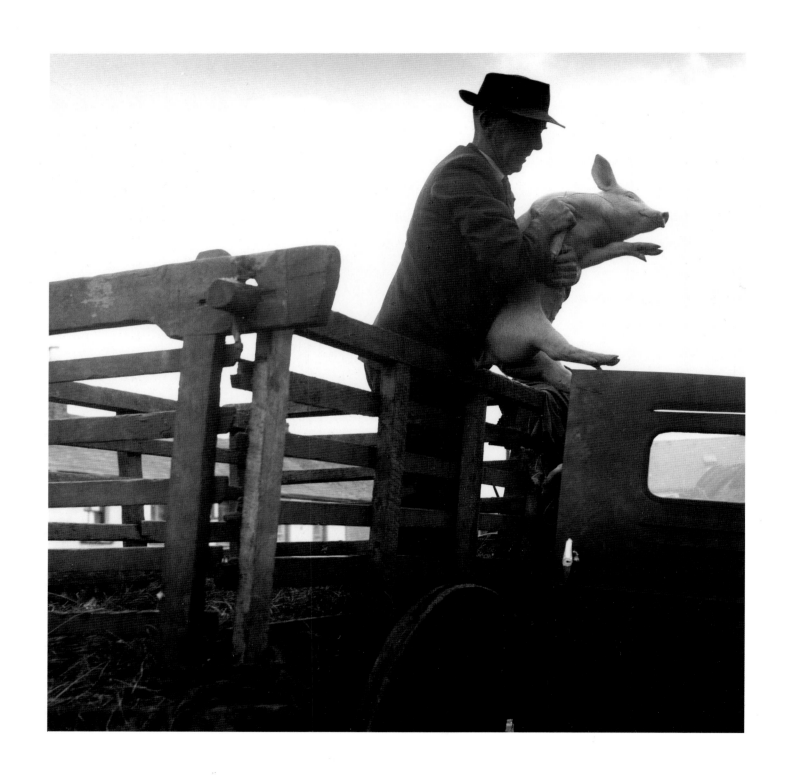

Bonhams *(young pigs), are commonly sold at the Ennis market.*

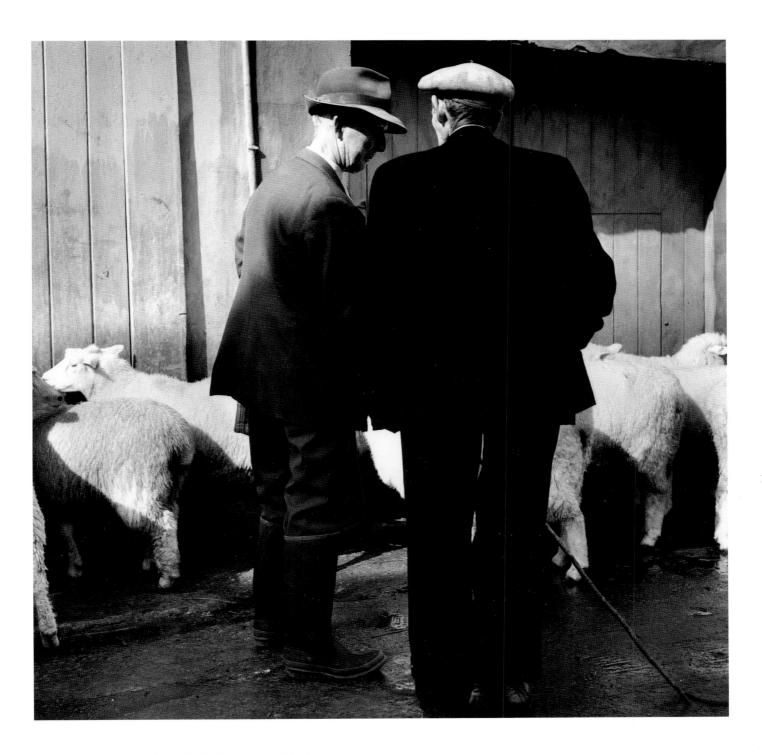

Negotiating the price of sheep may involve a lengthy discussion on unrelated topics such as sports, local gossip, and the weather before returning to the matter at hand.

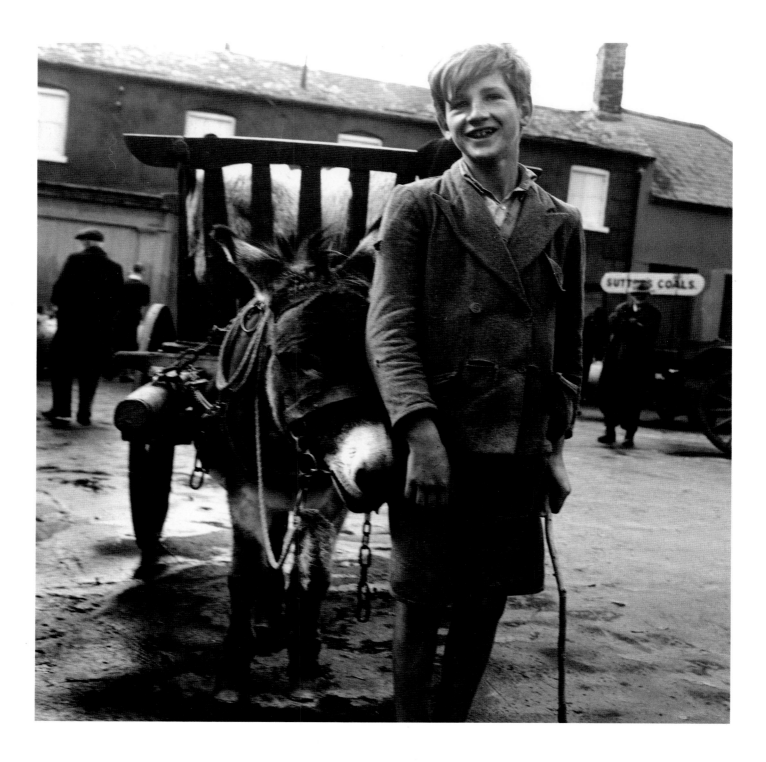

A boy watches over a creel loaded with recently purchased sheep at the Ennis market.

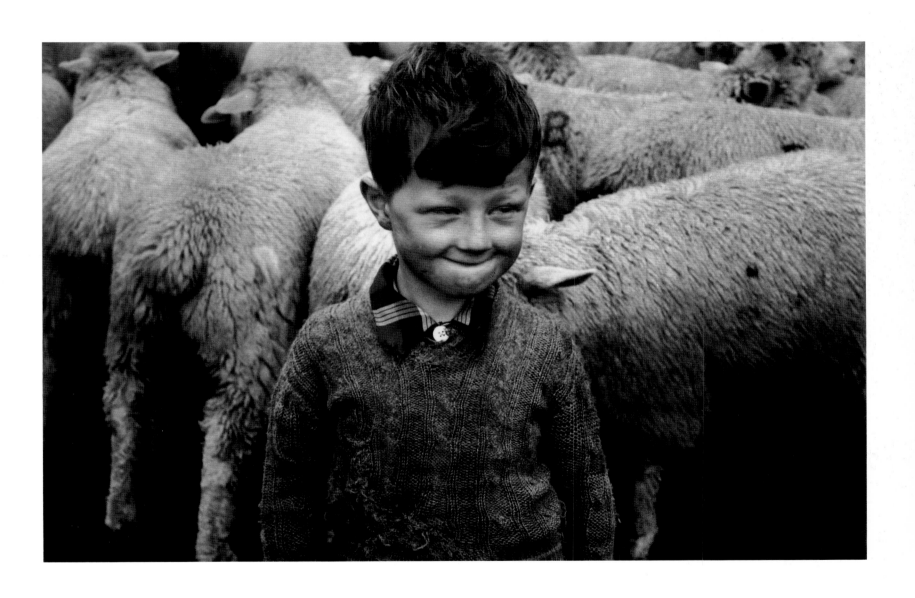

The Irish sometimes call a boy like this a "manín" (pronounced maneen), meaning a little man.

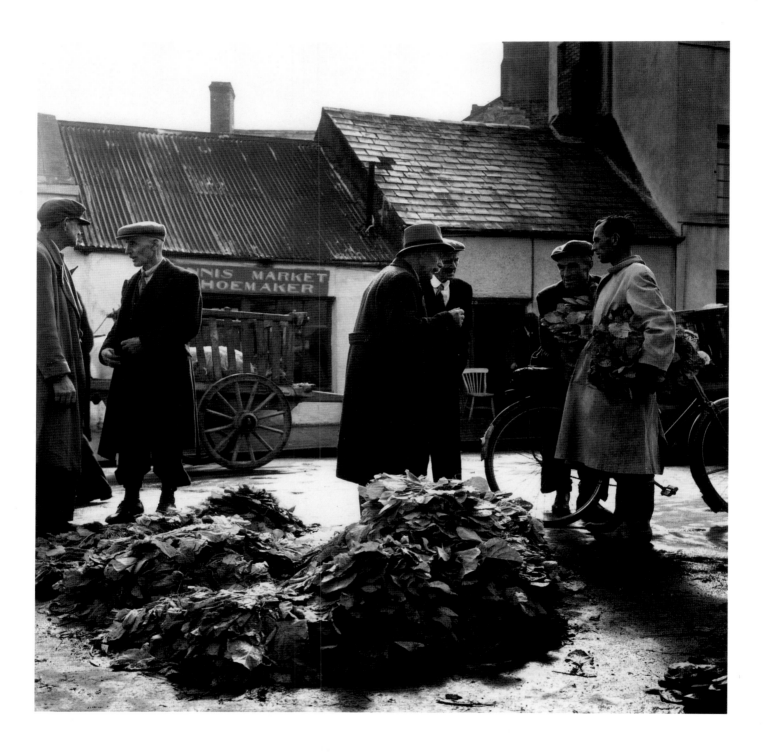

When cabbages propagated from seeds are about four months old, they are pulled and sold as cabbage plants, as seen here at The Mall in Ennis. They are then replanted by farmers who will later sell them as full heads of cabbage.

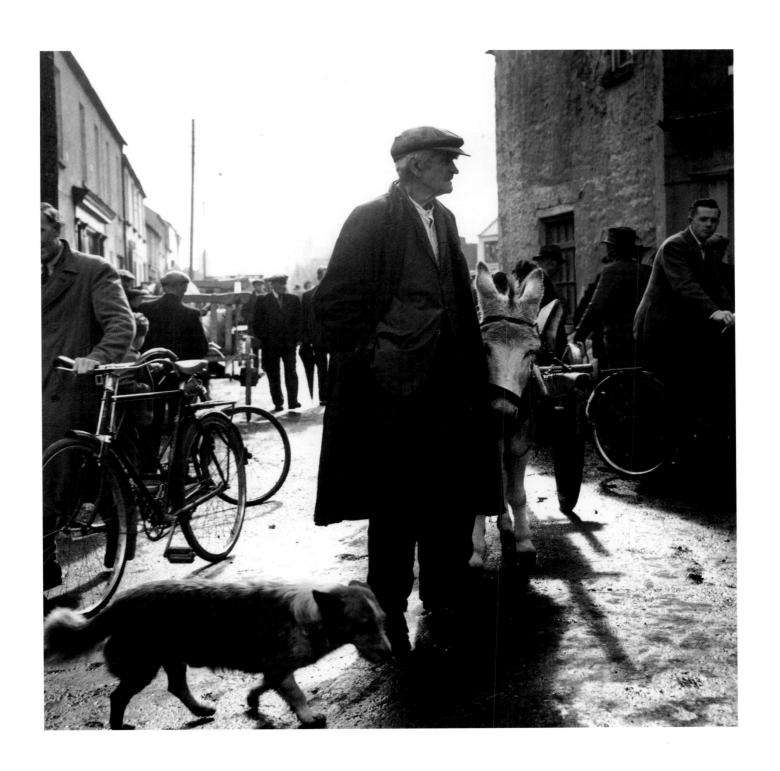

Forever the countryman's companion, this dog helps its owner make some purchasing decisions.

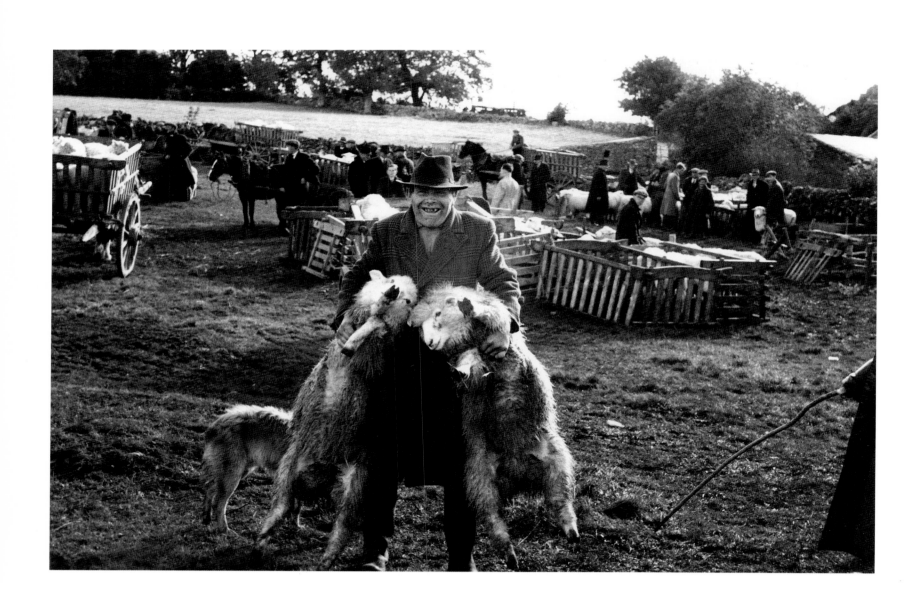

Paddy Flanagan of County Galway is less bashful in front of the camera than many of his farming friends. On this day, he has traveled to Tubber to examine some livestock.

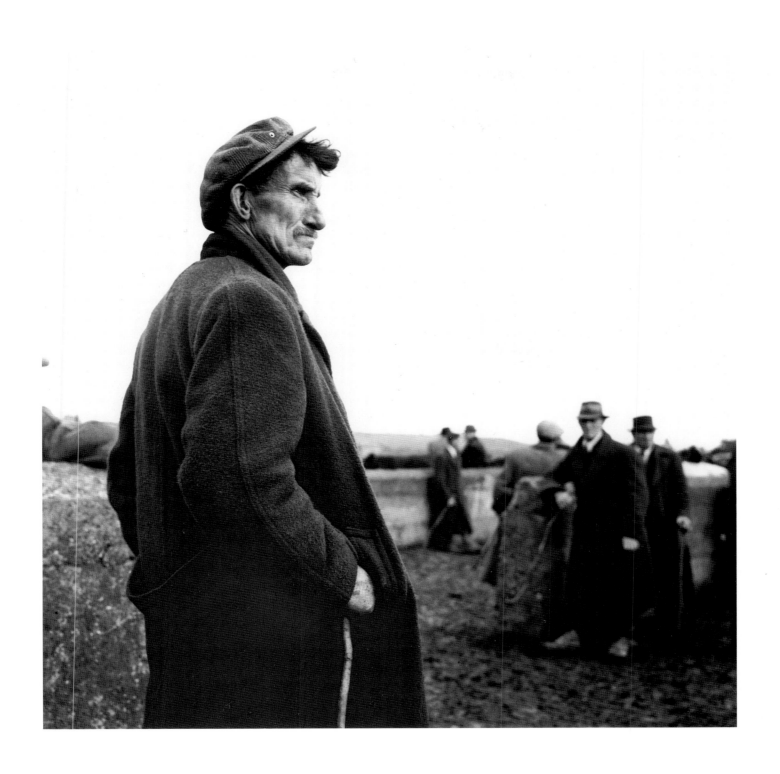

A farmer at the Tubber fair.

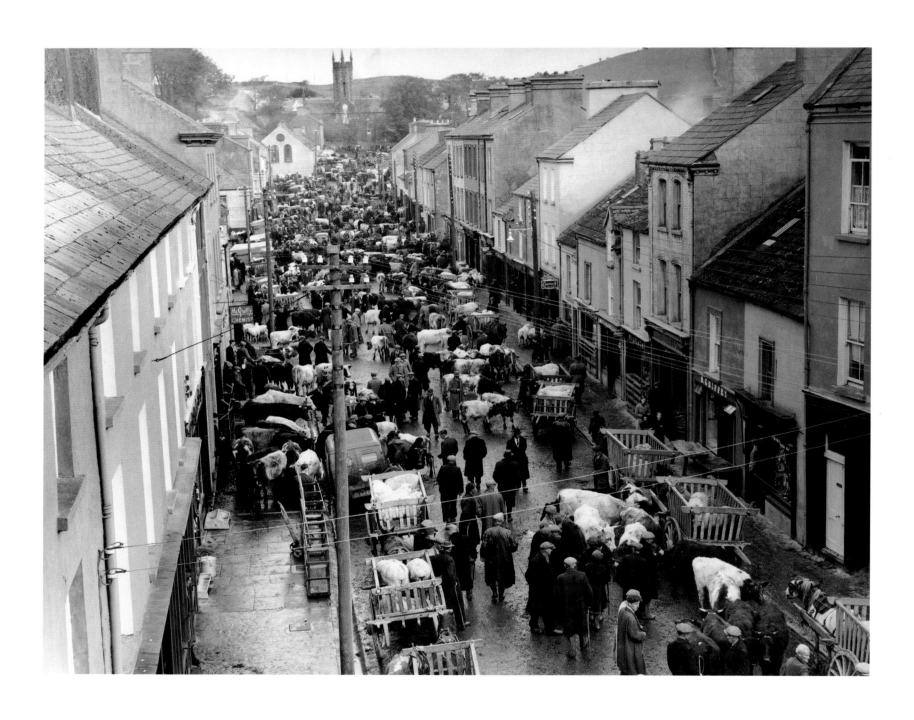

Ennistymon's Church Street, named for the Church of Ireland seen in the distance, is jammed once a month by frightened sheep, confused cattle, and the dealmakers who sell their livestock. The shops of Ennistymon are barricaded with pallets to prevent animals from crashing through their windows.

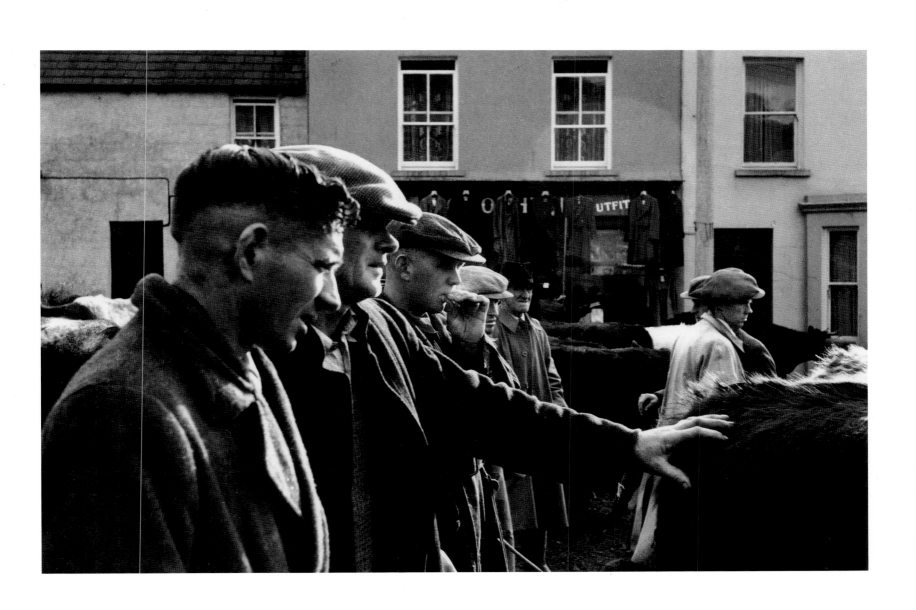

"Examining the rump" is the cattle buyer's equivalent of kicking tires in a car showroom.
No decisions will be made until the cattleman has checked the animal's conformation.

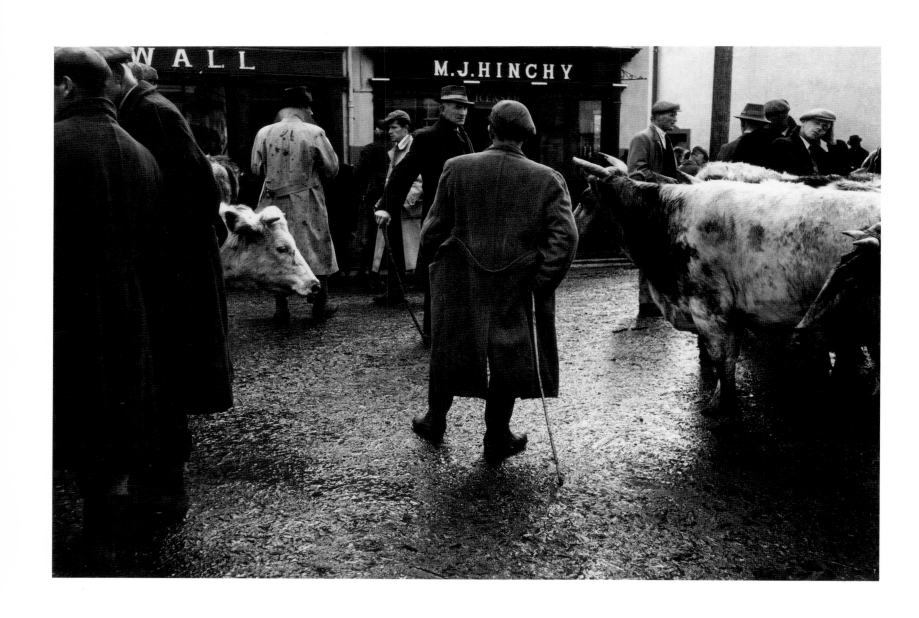

*A cap, a heavy coat, a hazel stick, and Wellington boots are standard garb for Irish farmers.
The monthly fair days are both a business and a social event, and later in the day after the
trading is done, Hinchy's pub is one of the local establishments that will benefit.*

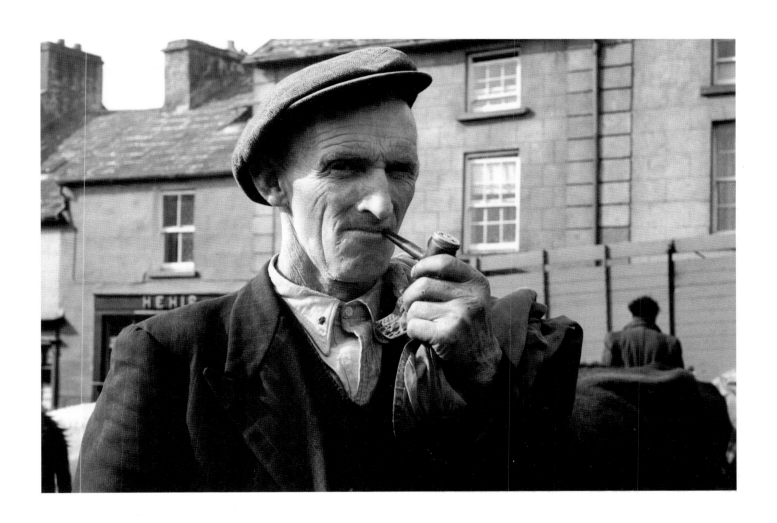

Paddy Reynolds from Kilfenora enjoys a draw on his pipe after driving his employer's cattle six miles to the Ennistymon fair. Known as a hard-living man, Paddy was popular with the local ladies in his youth but never married, a situation not helped by his landlessness.

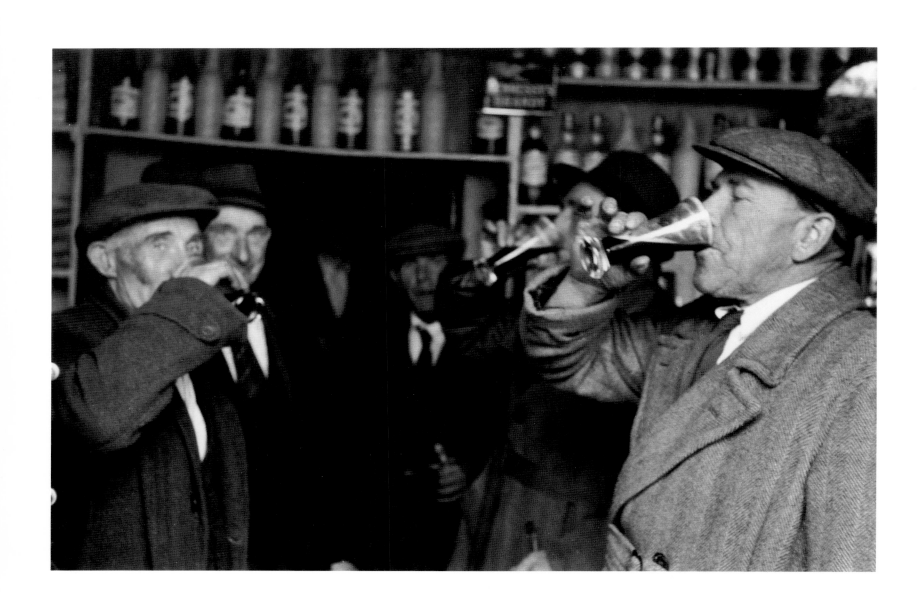

(Above and facing) Many of the cattle dealers have been on the road since 4:00 a.m. By midday, most of the deals have been done, leaving ample time for "a few jars" before the journey home.

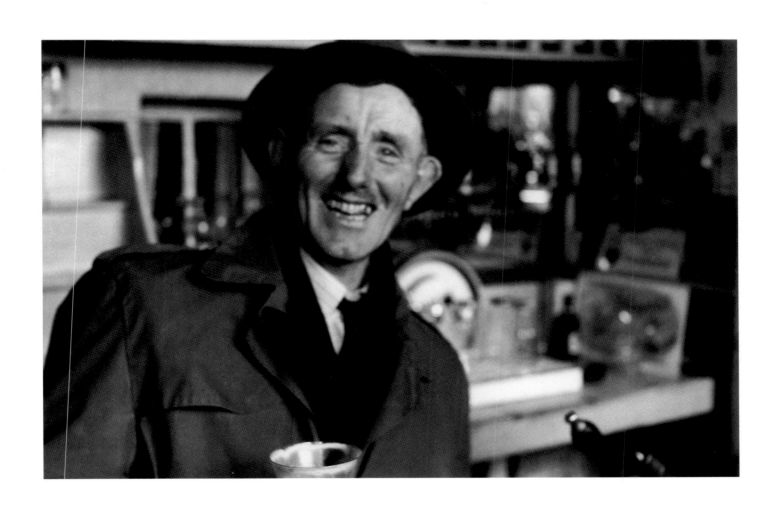

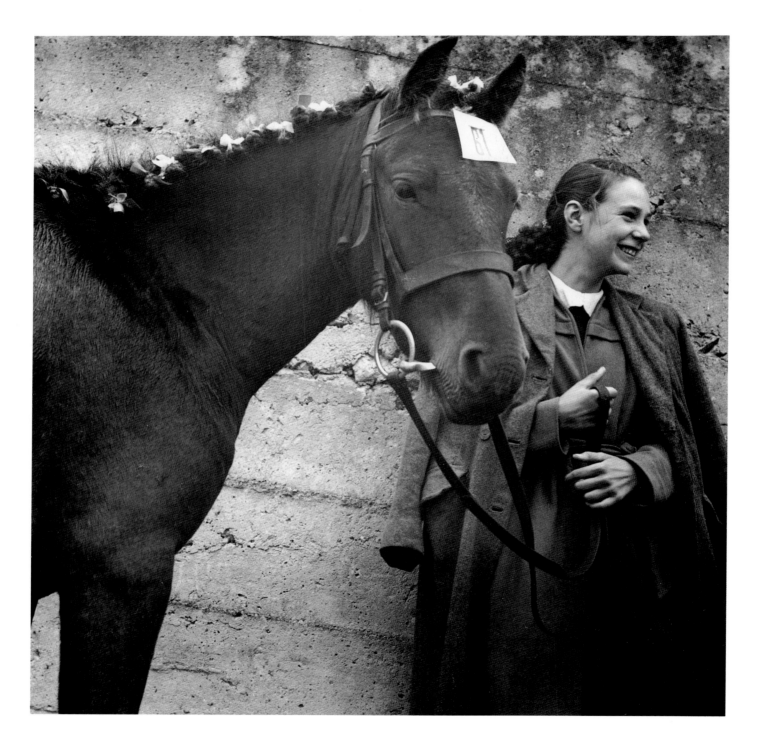

Equestrian competitions are a common feature at agricultural shows,
where the grooming of horse and rider are equally important.

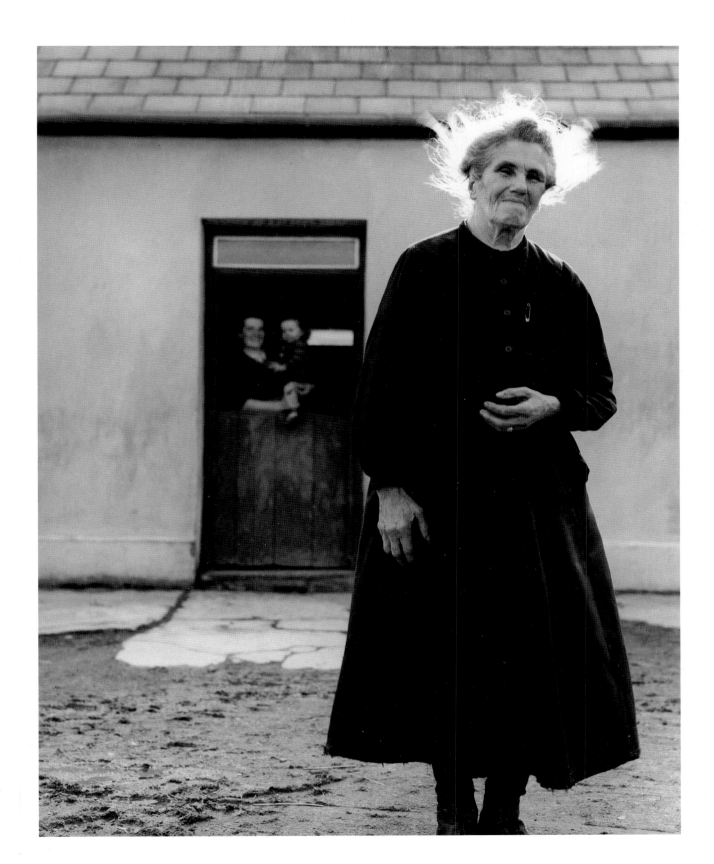

Mrs. Devitt from Knockature, Inagh, enjoys the fresh air behind her house, while her daughter-in-law Nonie and her grandchild look on.

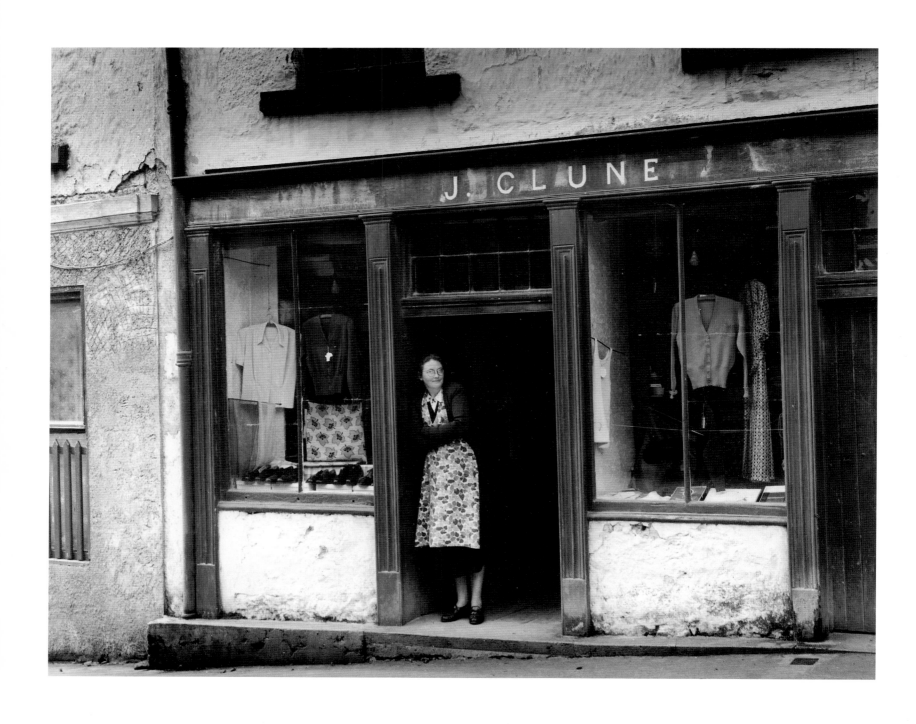

Clune's shop on the hill of Tulla.

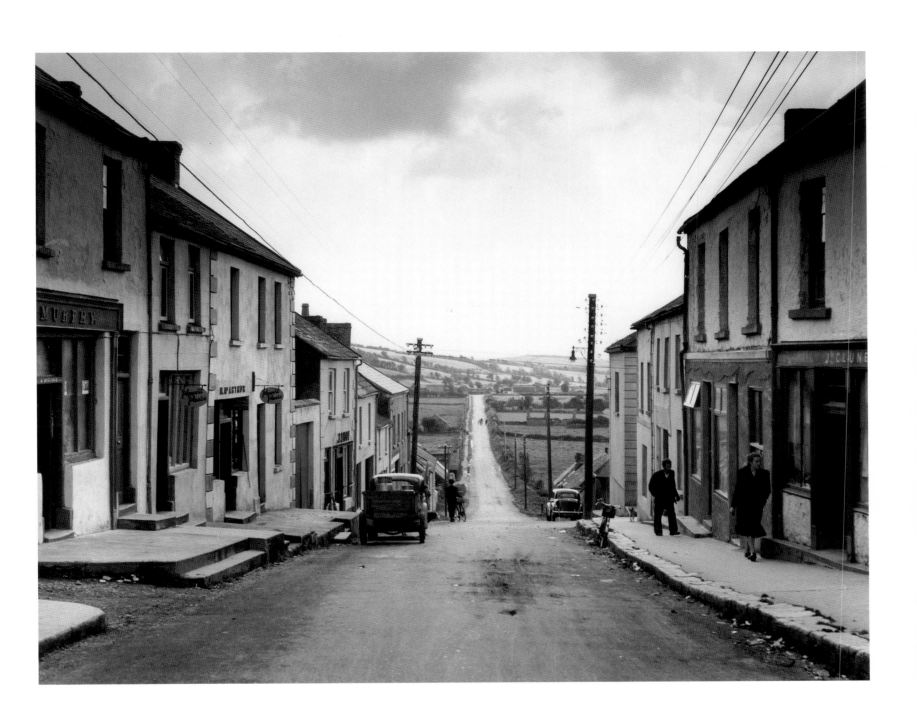

Main Street of the East Clare village of Tulla. The name comes from the word Tulach *meaning a hill. This, however, is a shortened version of its full name,* Tulach na nAspal, *"the hill of the apostles," or* Tulach na nEaspag, *"the hill of the bishops."*

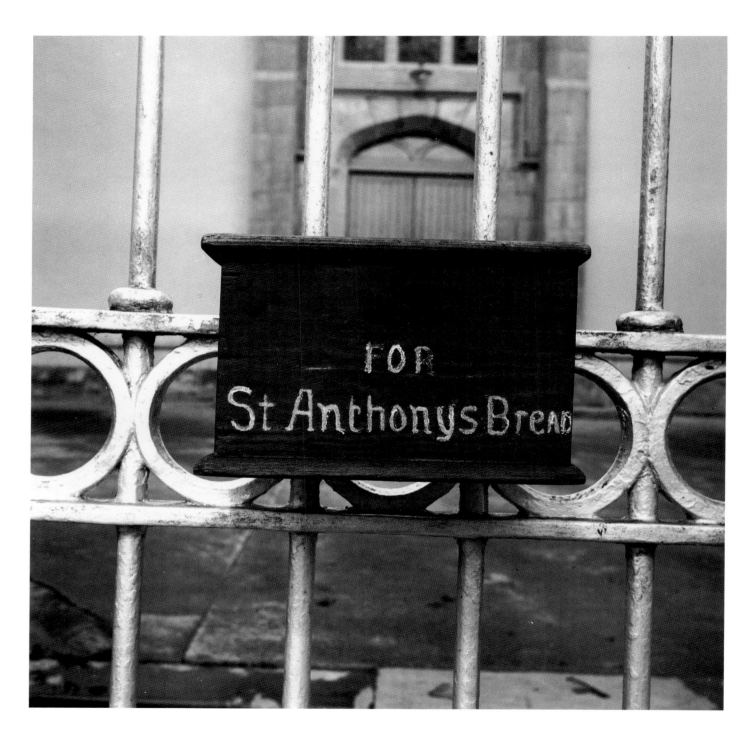

On the gate of Tulla church, donations for distribution among the local
poor are accepted in the name of St. Anthony.

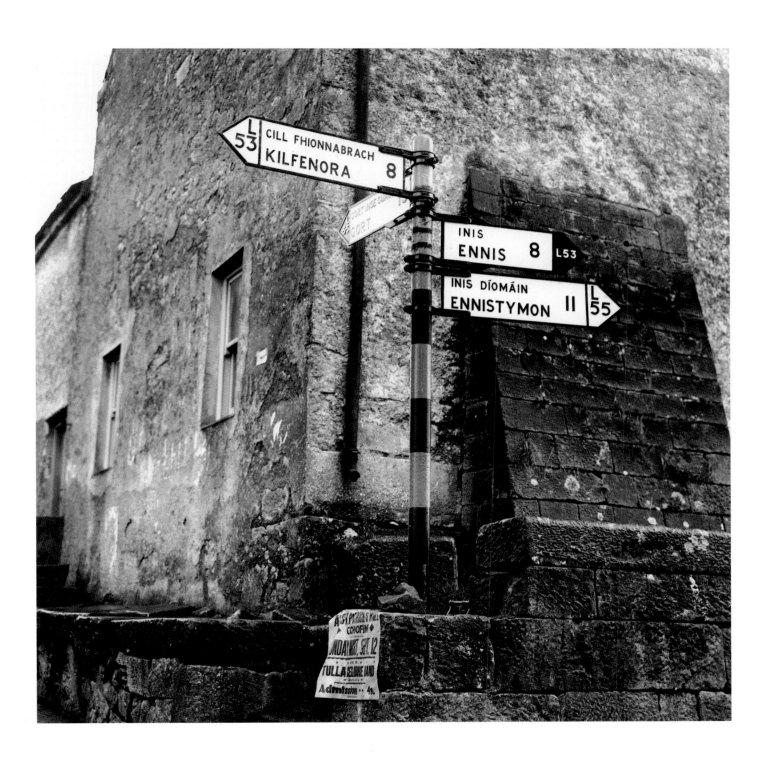

*A signpost in Corofin gives the original Irish name in smaller writing
above the commonly used English derivative.*

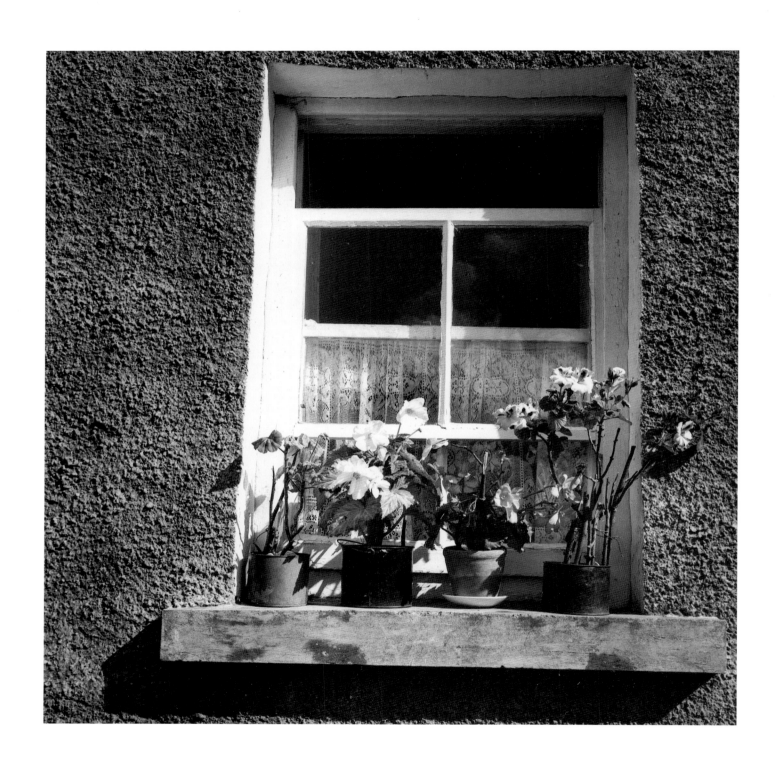

A windowsill adorned with geraniums and begonias.

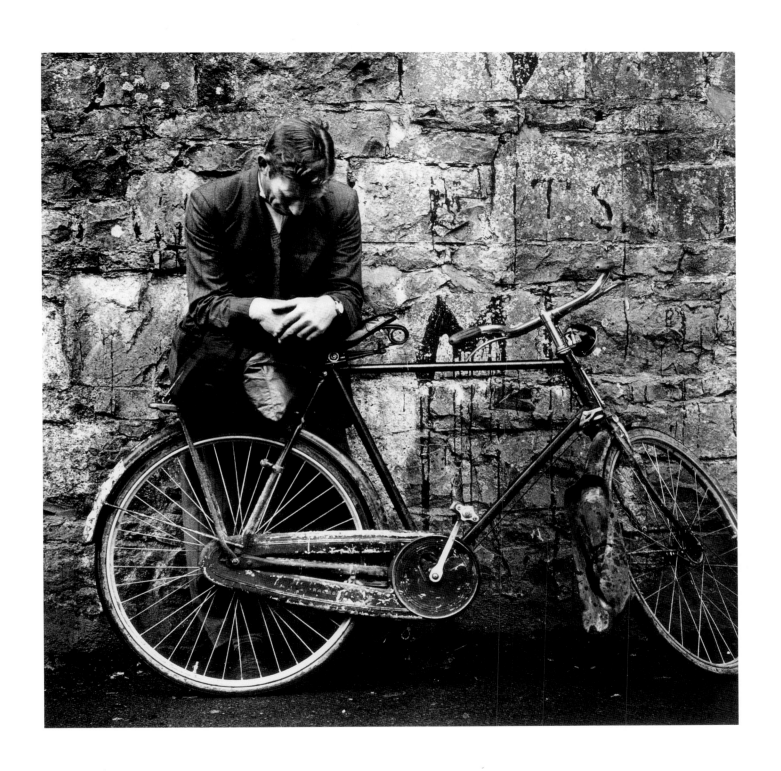

A young man pauses at the wall surrounding Rath church.

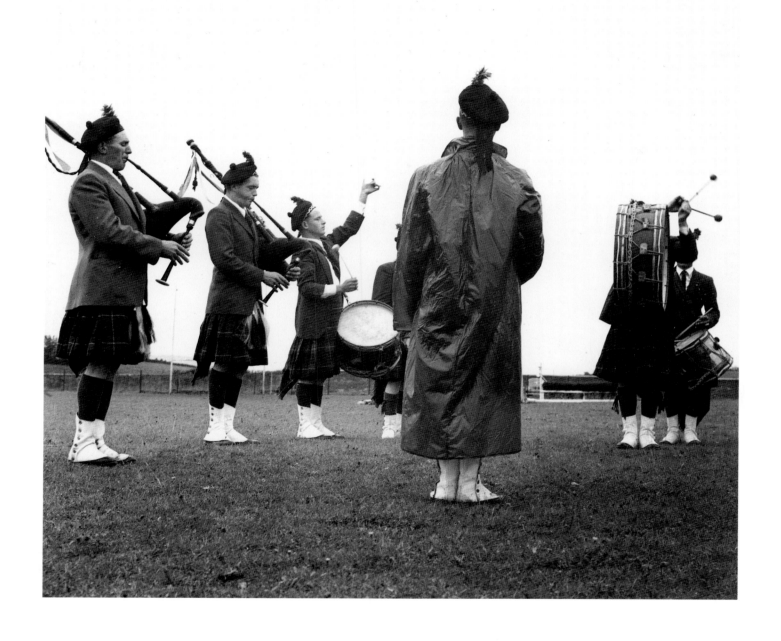

Pipe bands are common in towns throughout Ireland.

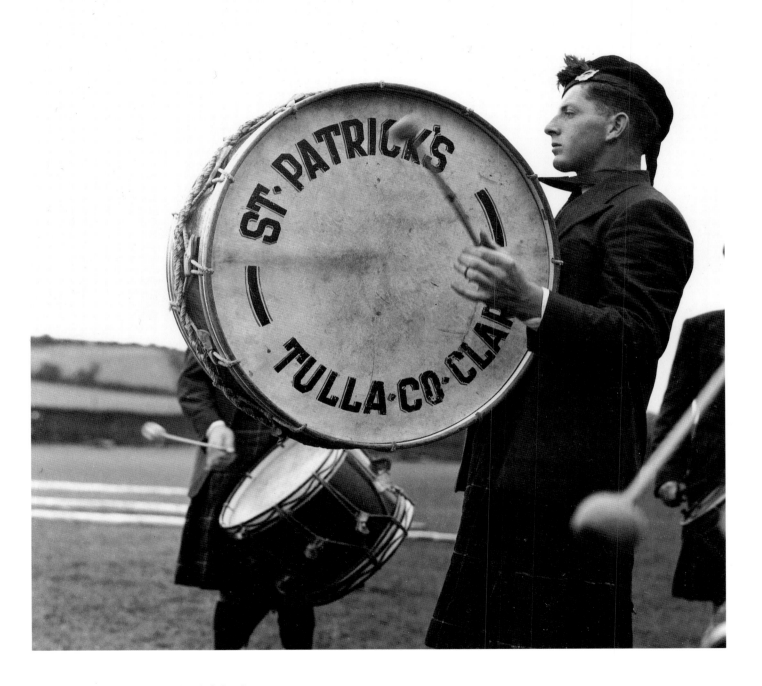

John O'Halloran of Rannagh, Tulla, beats a drum for St. Patrick's, a
pipe band founded in 1936 and still in existence today.

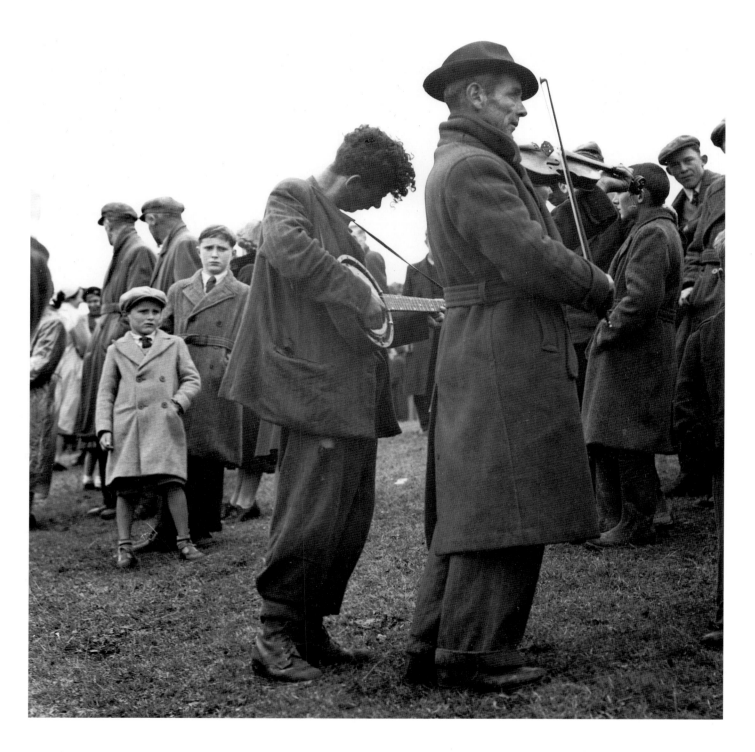

*The Dunne brothers of Limerick, one of whom is blind, are well-known for busking
at fairs, markets, and in this case a hurling match.*

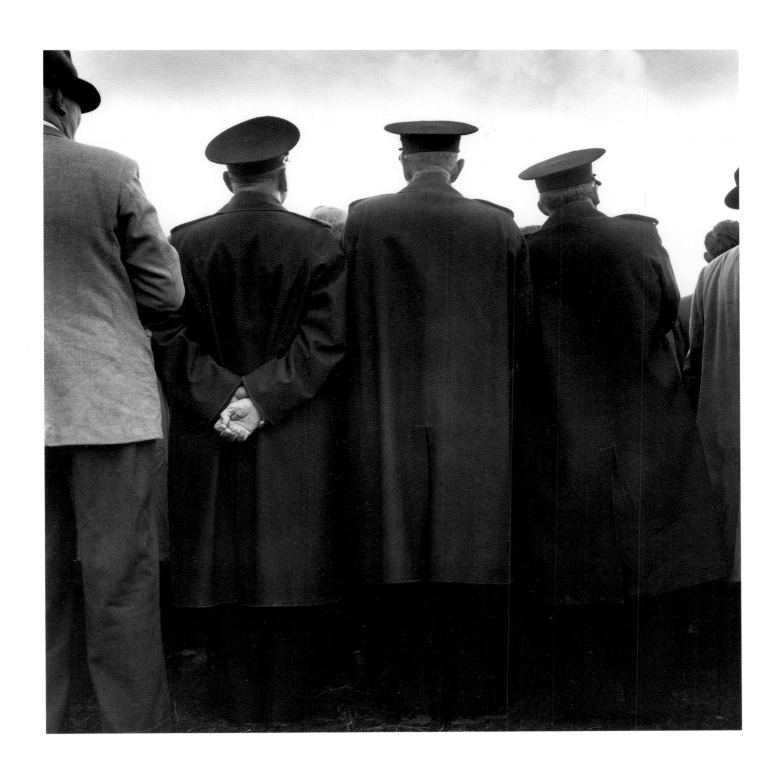

Members of the Garda Síochána *(Irish Police) enjoy the Sunday afternoon Gaelic games.*

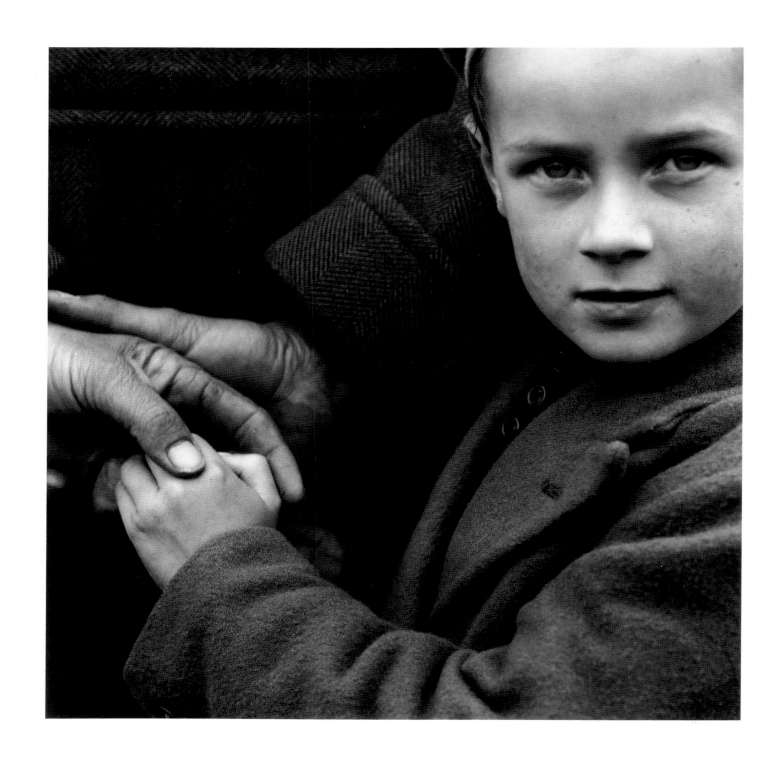

Hand in hand, a father and child attend a hurling game.

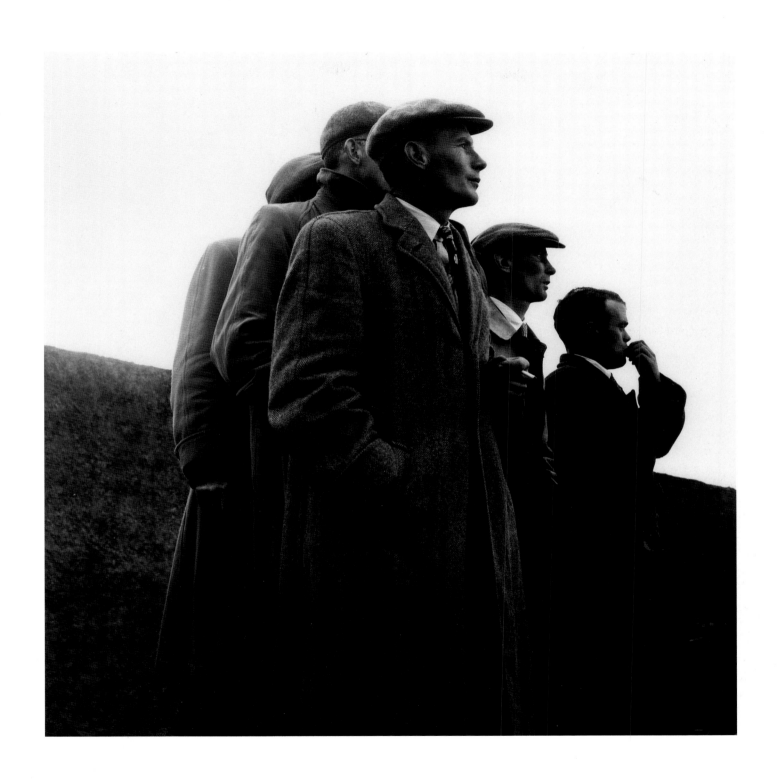

Sunday afternoon hurling absorbs the attention of the parish's men.

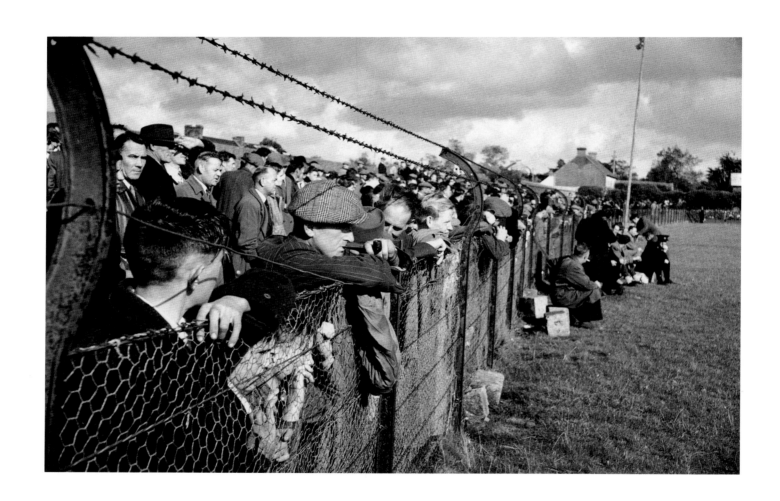

Spectators watch a hurling match at Father Murphy Memorial Park, Newmarket-on-Fergus.

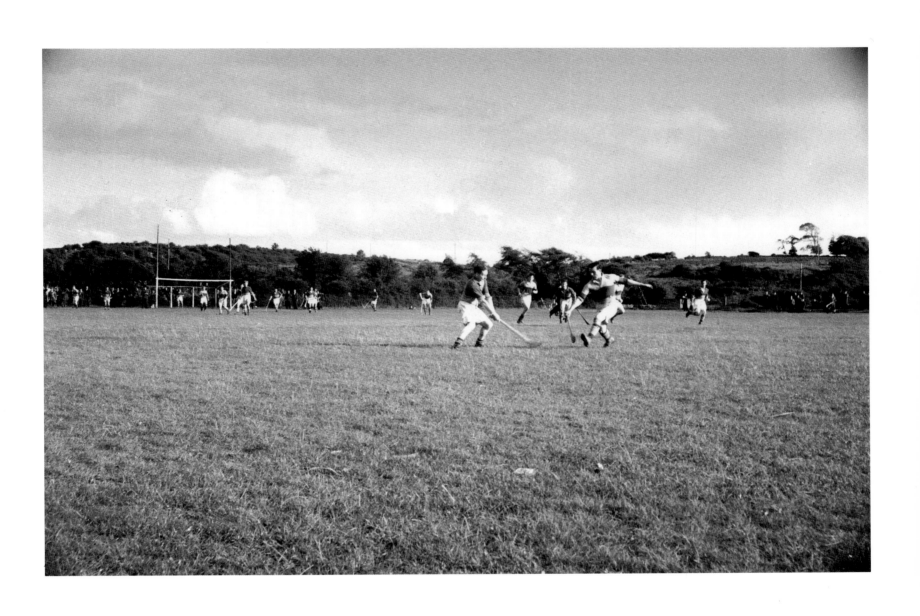

The object of hurling is to hit a small, hard leather ball called a sliotar (pronounced "slither")
between the poles of the H-shaped structure in the distance.

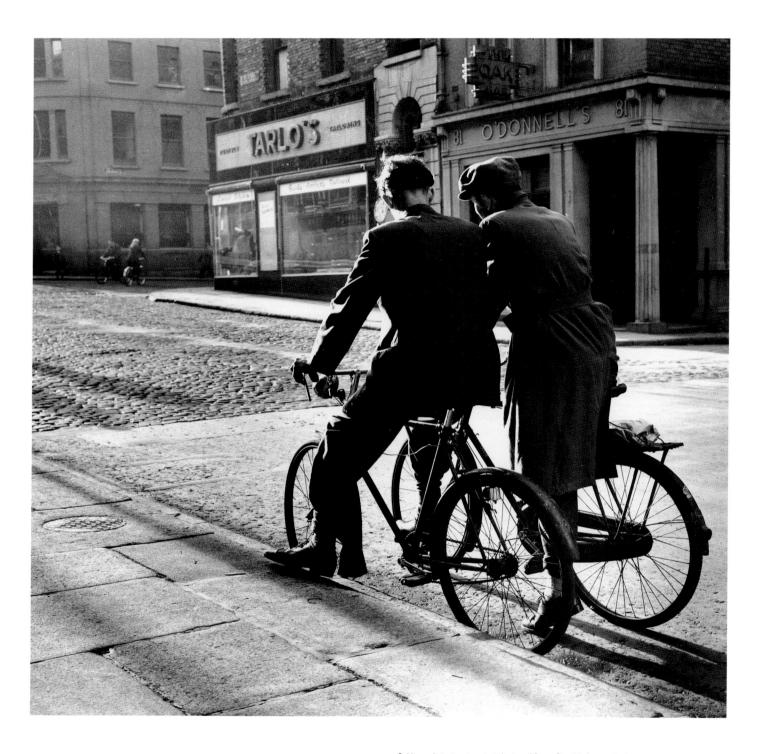

Dublin cyclists stop to rest at the top of Dame Street before continuing
their journey on an old cobblestone road, once the norm in every town and city.

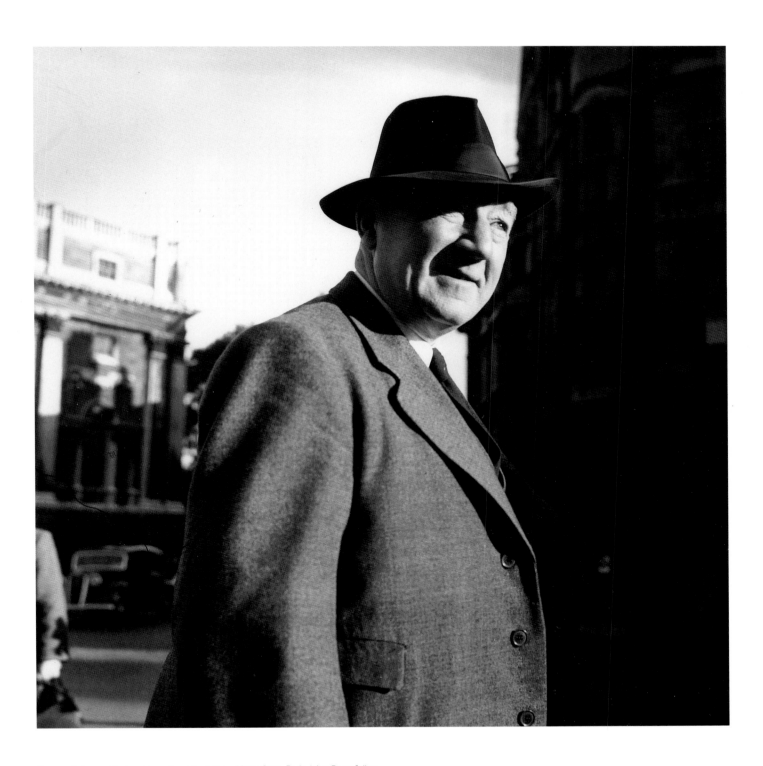

*A man waits to cross the busy intersection at the bottom of Dame Street. To the left is Trinity College
Dublin, built in 1592, and alma mater to such famous literary figures as Oscar Wilde and Samuel Beckett.*

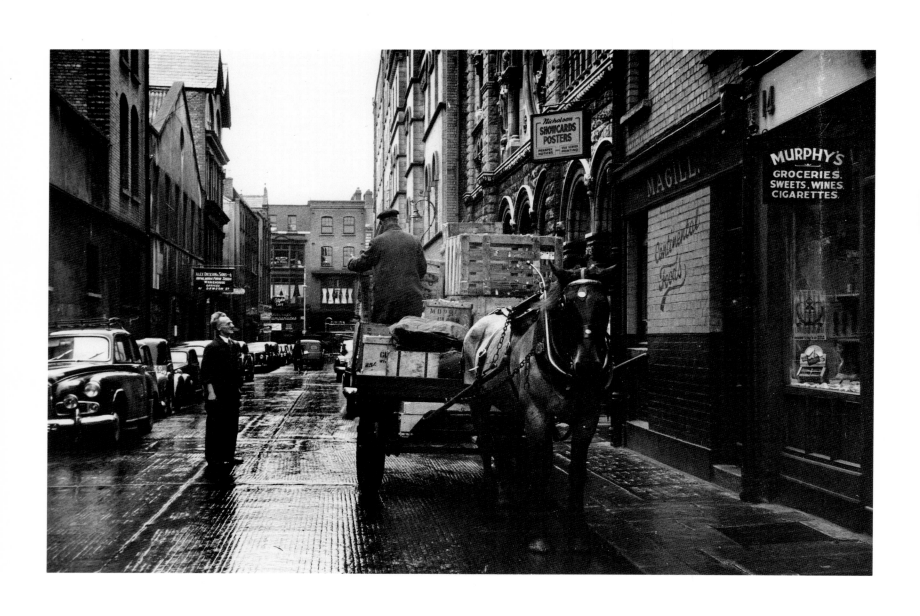

*A side road near Grafton Street is still wet from a recent downpour
as a Dublin deliveryman stops for a chat.*

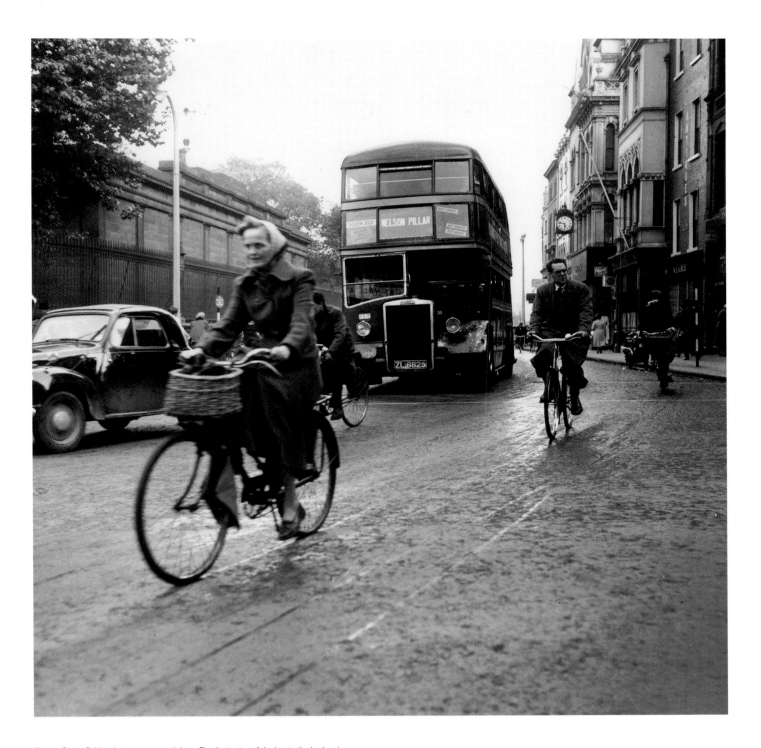

Nassau Street, Dublin, during evening rush hour. The destination of the bus is the landmark
Nelson Pillar, which was destroyed in an act of anti-British protest in 1966.

DOROTHEA LANGE BIOGRAPHY

By the time Dorothea Lange reached Ireland in 1954, she was a highly regarded documentary photographer, most noted for her work during the Great Depression. At age 59, she was also a grandmother and a veteran of several severe illnesses that had prevented her from working for most of the previous eight years.

Dorothy Nutzhorn, a child of German ancestry, was born in Hoboken, New Jersey, on May 26, 1895. Seven years

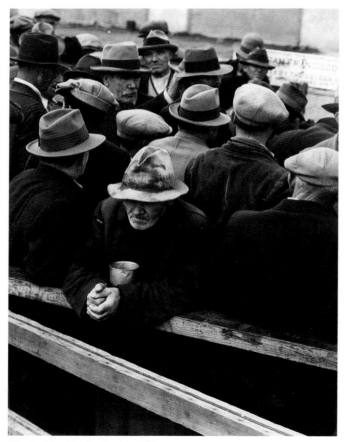

White Angel Breadline, *San Francisco, 1933.*

later, she contracted polio and was left with a painful life-long limp. At age 17, although she had never before taken a picture, she decided to become a professional photographer. She took a course and an apprenticeship in photography in New York before moving to San Francisco in 1919. There, Dorothy became Dorothea, and she shed the name of her estranged father, Nutzhorn, for that of her mother, Lange.

Within a year, Dorothea Lange established her own photographic studio. It was here that she met her first husband, Maynard Dixon, a maverick painter of the American West. They were married in 1920 and had two sons, Daniel (1925) and John (1928).

In 1932, restless with the portrait studio environment, she took her first set of photographs of the Great Depression. One of Lange's most popular images, *White Angel Breadline*, was made the very day she began photographing the subjects that were to make her famous. Never before had she worked in the field of documentary photography. She would spend the rest of her life serving this discipline and is credited as being one of its creators.

In 1935, following an exhibition of her street photography, she met Dr. Paul Taylor, then an associate professor of economics at the nearby University of California at Berkeley. He was also Field Director of the State Emergency Relief Administration (SERA) of California, and together they were to work on many projects relating to migrant farm labor, with him interviewing migrants and writing reports on their conditions, and her providing pictures to accompany his text. Their efforts led directly to the establishment of federally sponsored camps for displaced people. They divorced their respective partners in 1935, and married in a quiet ceremony in New Mexico that same year.

Taylor arranged for Lange to become the official photographer for SERA. This led to a position at the Farm Security Administration (FSA), where for five years she photographed the tide of economic refugees entering California, victims of the Depression and the Dust Bowl.

During this time, Lange produced some of her most famous work, including the *Migrant Mother*, one of the most widely reproduced photographs ever. Her work also inspired other artists, most notably John Steinbeck, whose novel *The Grapes of Wrath*, and the subsequent movie version, drew on her images.

In 1940 Lange and Taylor produced their book, *American Exodus: A Record of Human Erosion*, which received praise for highlighting so well the tragedy of the dispossessed farm worker. The following year, she became the first woman to receive the prestigious Guggenheim Fellowship, a grant that enables outstanding artists to devote a full year to creative work. She used the grant to support her study of contrasting religious communities, which focused on the

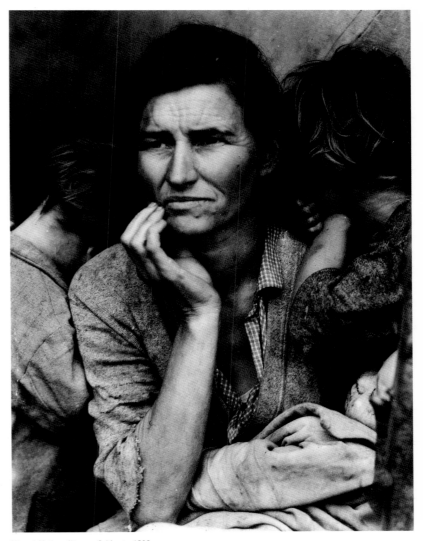

Migrant Mother, *Nipomo, California, 1936.*

Hutterites in South Dakota and the Amana Society in Iowa.

Starting in 1942, and continuing for 18 months, she photographed the execution of Executive Order 9066, which saw the internment of 110,000 innocent Japanese–Americans for the duration of World War II. Although she had been hired by the War Relocation Authority to be its official photographer, she was outspoken in her opposition to the internment and complained of rough treatment from the American military while she was working on the project.

Shortly afterward, she became ill with ulcers and gallbladder trouble. From 1945 to 1950, it was uncertain if she would survive her illnesses, and she took few photographs. She recommenced her Guggenheim work in 1951, and in 1953 did a study of Mormon life in Utah with Ansel Adams and her son Daniel Dixon. She was, in the opinion of Daniel, now a better photographer than ever before.

In 1954 she and Daniel again worked together, this time in Ireland, on an assignment from *Life* magazine. It was her first time outside the United States, and she liked the country and the people. She took 2,400 pictures while in Ireland and was very pleased with the work she did there.

After Ireland, she worked on other photographic essays including "The Public Defender," an exploration of the American legal system from the defendant's point of view, and "The Barryessa Valley," a documentation of the destruction of a California valley to make way for a reservoir. Her pictures were also included in Edward Steichen's celebrated "The Family of Man" exhibition for the Museum of Modern Art, which opened in New York in the fall of 1952 and was eventually seen by more than 90 million people in 70 countries worldwide.

Between 1958 and 1963, Lange traveled with Paul Taylor to Asia, South America, North Africa, and the Middle East and Far East. Their schedule was set by Paul's rural development work for organizations such as the United Nations, and as a result, Dorothea's work suffered. In Egypt, she was frustrated to the point of tears by the hostility she faced from villagers who were fearful that she was taking pictures for the Israeli government.

For most of her life, those who knew her best both respected and feared Dorothea Lange's unyielding nature. Her strength of character powered this independent, semicrippled woman through physically tough field trips and preserved her spirit during the most painful of illnesses and treatments. But her powerful personality was also well-known for pulling her into bitter battles with family and colleagues.

Her iron will was tested again after the summer of 1964, when she was diagnosed as having cancer of the esophagus. She decided to work as best she could on two remaining projects: a documentary film on her life that she had agreed to make with KQED, a San Francisco educational TV station, and a major retrospective exhibition of her work at the Museum of Modern Art. She completed the documentary, but on October 11, 1965, she died at her home in Berkeley, while finishing preparations for her retrospective exhibition. The exhibition of 87 prints opened in New York three months later and included five previously unpublished pictures from her work in Ireland.